Poland/1931

Also by Jerome Rothenberg

Poems

White Sun Black Sun (1960)
The Seven Hells of the Jigoku Zoshi (1962)
Sightings I-IX (1964)
The Gorky Poems (1966)
Between: Poems 1960–1963 (1967)
Conversations (1968)
Poems 1964–1967 (1968)
Poland / 1931, first installment (1969)
A Book of Testimony (1971)
Poems for the Game of Silence (1971)
Seneca Journal I: A Poem of Beavers (1973)
The Cards (1974)
Esther K. Comes to America (1974)

Translations

New Young German Poets (1959)
Hochhuth's "The Deputy," playing version (1965)
Enzensberger's "Poems for People Who Don't Read Poems," with Michael
      Hamburger (1968)
The Book of Hours & Constellations, or Gomringer by Rothenberg (1968)
The 17 Horse-Songs of Frank Mitchell X-XIII (1970)

Anthologies

Ritual (1966)
Technicians of the Sacred (1968)
Shaking the Pumpkin (1971)
America a Prophecy, with George Quasha (1973)
Revolution of the Word (1974)

Poland/1931

JEROME ROTHENBERG

A New Directions Book

ACKNOWLEDGMENTS

Grateful acknowledgment is made to the editors and publishers of magazines and books in which some of the material in this volume previously appeared: *America a Prophecy* (Jerome Rothenberg and George Quasha, eds.: New York, Random House), *American Literary Anthology 3* (George Plimpton and Peter Ardery, eds.: New York, The Viking Press), *Anonym, Catalogue* (London, Modern American Poetry Conference, 1973), *Caterpillar, A Caterpillar Anthology* (Clayton Eshleman, ed.: New York, Doubleday), *Choice, Corpus, Coyote's Journal, Damascus Road, European Judaism* (London), *Ikon, Imago* (Montreal), *Intrepid, Io, Laugh Literary and Man the Humping Guns, The Nation, New Directions in Prose and Poetry 28, Open Poetry* (Ronald Gross and George Quasha, eds.: New York, Simon & Schuster), *Poetry Review* (London); *Preferences* (Thomas Victor, ed.: New York, The Viking Press), *Raster* (Holland), *Response, Sixpack, some/thing, Stony Brook, Sumac, Tractor, Transpacific, Tree, Unmuzzled Ox.*

Portions of this book appeared in previous collections by Jerome Rothenberg and are reprinted here by permission of the publishers: The Dial Press (*Poems for the Game of Silence 1960–1970*), Tree Books (*A Book of Testimony*), and Unicorn Press (*Esther K. Comes to America* and *Poland/1931*).

Illustration credits: collage (1967) facing page 1 by Eleanor Antin; photograph, page 28, by Laurence Fink; postal cards, pages 48 and 100, and collage, page 82, courtesy of the author; artwork, page 120, by the author; artwork, page 140, by Michael Manfredo.

Manufactured in the United States of America
First published clothbound and as New Directions Paperbook 379 in 1974
Published simultaneously in Canada by McClelland & Stewart, Ltd.

Library of Congress Cataloging in Publication Data

Rothenberg, Jerome, 1931–
    Poland/1931.

    (A New Directions Book)
    Poems.
    I. Title.
PS3568.086P6   811'.5'4   74–8646
ISBN 0–8112–0541–X
ISBN 0–8112–0542–8 (pbk.)

New Directions Books are published for James Laughlin
by New Directions Publishing Corporation,
333 Sixth Avenue, New York 10014

For my son Matthew
("The Speaker")
with whom I learned to sing

. . . And I said, "O defiled flock, take a harp, &
chant to the ancient relics, lest understanding
perish."   —E. DAHLBERG

CONTENTS

Poland / 1931

my mind is stuffed with tablecloths
& with rings but my mind
is dreaming of poland stuffed with poland
brought in the imagination
to a black wedding
a naked bridegroom hovering above
his naked bride   mad poland
how terrible thy jews at weddings
thy synagogues with camphor smells & almonds
thy thermos bottles thy electric fogs
thy braided armpits
thy underwear alive with roots o poland
poland poland poland poland poland
how thy bells wrapped in their flowers toll
how they do offer up their tongues to kiss the moon
old moon old mother stuck in thy sky thyself
an old bell with no tongue a lost udder
o poland thy beer is ever made of rotting bread
thy silks are linens merely thy tradesmen
dance at weddings where fanatic grooms
still dream of bridesmaids still are screaming
past their red moustaches poland
we have lain awake in thy soft arms forever
thy feathers have been balm to us
thy pillows capture us like sickly wombs & guard us
let us sail through thy fierce weddings poland
let us tread thy markets where thy sausages grow ripe & full
let us bite thy peppercorns let thy oxen's dung be sugar to
        thy dying jews
o poland o sweet resourceful restless poland
o poland of the saints unbuttoned poland repeating endlessly
        the triple names of mary
poland poland poland poland poland
have we not tired of thee poland no for thy cheeses
shall never tire us nor the honey of thy goats

3

thy grooms shall work ferociously upon their looming brides
shall bring forth executioners
shall stand like kings inside thy doorways
shall throw their arms around thy lintels poland
& begin to crow

THE KING OF THE JEWS

Is a stranger. Is
Sharp. Cries
For fish. Is wanting
A wristwatch.

A Poultice. One
Bathes. One intrudes
On the Nightwatch.
One steals.

Catch him. He slips
From your nets. Anoint
Him. The father of weights.
Brother of Edom.

One is a practical man.
One protects. One
Gathers. The table is set.
Find platters.

Find ostriches. Hair
Is refinement.
For thieves. For widows.
A stitch is copper.

One cuts. Makes fingers
That button. He
Suits us. Soon
He is fed.

He is heavy. One
Sings for him. Bathes
In his room.
One counts sheets for him.

Is a steward. Is
Dull. Begs
For soup. Is wanting
A hatband.

One steals. One adds numbers.
He testifies. What
Is a number past one.
A number.

THE KEY OF SOLOMON

tallow tongues of oxen cock messias sorrel pox a glass
a root a dish an open dish a cockatrice a ring a key:

From the skin of a hare
the blood of a black hen
or a newly killed sheep
& occasionally the meat of animals & birds
the food is steamed with pleasant odors.
Stand at the eastern corner.
Bless this carpet.
Burn a dove's feather.
Point to westward.

Afflict the knees
& tyrannize over cats.
This is the ring of travel.
This is the yellow cloth
that causes love between two people.
From this will be made an ink.
From this a square.
A turtle.
Take a chain, a hook & the figure of a bird.
Make a talisman of leather.
& a white vessel.
This is the ring of incest
"the needle of the art."
Its signs are seven.

> *Saturn, black.*
> *Jupiter, azure blue.*
> *Mars, red.*
> *Sun, gold or yellow.*
> *Venus, green.*
> *Mercury, mixed.*
> *Moon, silver or white grey.*

& it is said in The Book of Beasts
that the lizard fleeth the privvy members of a man
therefore when they see it
they bind ropes from the male to the female
& bow down to the male.

SATAN IN GORAY

A Homage to Isaac Bashevis Singer

1

Sect.
Avert sect.
Avert to wash bellies.
Sect.
Avert sect.

2

Worship.
Womanly
Towns & Towns.
Tones.
Witness.
Witness & Witness.
Woman redeemed.

Woman redeemed woman redeemed.

3

Crutches.
Crutches cockcrow.
Crutches cockcrow Jews.
Crutches impure.
Crutches impure cockcrow.
Crutches Jews.

4

Drinking.
Drinking in devil.
Prayers.
Prayerful.

5

Messiah.
First a holiday malice.
Abyss.
Ark bares Levi.

6

Sabbath.
Sabbatai Zevi.
Sodom Sodom.
Sodom Sodom.

7

Marriage bed marriage bed.
Brittle.
Marriage breasts.
Marriage breasts bristle.
Match me.
Onan.
Again.
Pederasty.
In Three.

8

Fat yes fat yes fat yes idol. Fat yes fat yes fat yes idol.

8

9

Something is Presence.

10

Holy Muhammed.

11

Pass over.
Pass over.
Pass.
Pass.
Pass.
Pass.
Pass pass.   (G. Stein)

Pass water.

12

Lilith a red head.
Jest nudgingly.
S & Z & S & Z.   S & Z & S & Z.   S & Z & S & Z.   Selah.

SOAP (I)

The lonely. Sliding
between my hands
A sorrowful island
he dreams of small birds in fragments above his head
& smeared windows
misted eyeglasses
something white floating in a tumbler
lips drinking
remembering a silence white as soap
like rubbing out a name
"the man who writes his name
     on the beloved's belly"
knows it
what does the man know
hiding from a name?

Answer: "the place where it was hidden"

wax. Sweet
scent
an open skylight
soap
a hand against the tap, palm flat
delight of using soap
he opens papers
sometimes he throws away the ribbon
& picks his nose
Soap in all his orifices
he says, Someone
is clean
Even the doorknob smells of soap

SOAP (II)

Will the man who gets clean love his neighbor?
Yes the facts are apparent yes the facts
live on in the mind if the mind lives on
"I have no right to another man's business
& it makes me sick"
When Meyer fell asleep in his chair, his wife shouted DON'T
    TOUCH MEYER!
The sugar at the bottom of his cup was brown & hard
Twice a month he had the hairs clipped from his nose
& thanked his barber
(he had sold him shaving soap the day before)
Selling soap to the pious
calling it *zeyf*
saying: *ah shtick zeyf*
or saying: *ah shtickeleh zeyf* (dim.)
theirs was a business between friends
& meant lying
But the tips of his fingers smellt good to him
women admired it
the books on his shelf were in a language he couldn't
    understand
So he began to make little songs
& to stuff his pockets with little bars of soap
"Children, eat omelets
"Children, when the chamberpots are empty the great bear
    comes at night
"Children, there are other values in this life"
Yes said the voices in his dream yes
sang the voices to the man who sold soap
& was ticklish
But where will the road end, do the voices
tell you where the road will end
Do they lead you to a new town where the people aren't clean?
"I have no right to another man's business
& it makes me sick"
There were always towns like that

THE CONNOISSEUR OF JEWS

if there were locomotives to ride home on
& no jews
there would still be jews & locomotives
just as there are jews & oranges
& jews & jars
there would still be someone to write the jewish poem
others to write their mothers' names in light—
just as others, born angry
have the moon's face burnt onto their arms
& don't complain
my love, my lady, be a connoisseur of jews
the fur across your lap
was shedding
on the sheet were hairs
the first jew to come to you is mad
the train pulls into lodz
he calls you
by your polish name
then he tells the other passengers a story
there are jews & there are alphabets
he tells them
but there are also jewish alphabets
just as there are jewish locomotives
& jewish hair
& just as there are some with jewish fingers
such men are jews
just as other men are not jews
not mad
don't call you by your polish name
or ride the train to lodz
if there are men who ride the train to lodz
there are still jews
just as there are still oranges
& jars
there is still someone to write the jewish poem
others to write their mothers' names in light

THE MOTHERS

1

scandal, too hard to bear
but kept in her mind
from girlhood   it returned
& hung around the bed
somebody's mouth was always going
words in the old tongue
language of the simple people of our town
there ought to be a book
if someone would ever learn to write with light
& burn it in my heart
that was the way we learnt our history
but forgot it
learnt to unscramble simple sentences
& as a girl husht it up

2

mothers first
& dancers in love with misfortune
together we sat
together we told the bushes the names of our loves
a spy?
a squadron of guards from the palace?
a dirigible back of the lake?
all is secret, sing the mothers
all is innocent
& draws a white circle
behind their eyes
the circle starts to swell   moistens
& leaves a trail of fat
how beautiful, she says

3

she has their desire to be always in love
always respectable
as if prosperity were the name of a town
or of a house in the town
& had no windows
"doomed to old age, they withered"
went the song   the secret was out
there will be no sun from this day forward
no more numbers to add up
or coins embedded in the risen dough
all is done, sing the mothers
all is forgiven
& has no book of its own written in light
& no town

the dead fish has no eyes
says my son, poland
has no eyes
& so we live without associations
in the past we live
nourishing incredible polands
lazy & alive remembering
our mothers' pictures in the grass
this is the jewish poem
not being jewish much less
being polish
much less being human
we are miles away
& we move toward something unmistakably
alive & fat
a tender treasure an illusion
how clean we are
we sing   the fathers
having once been insistent
now turn deaf
they open stores in kansas
dream of links
to china secret cargoes
with a mad impulse to buy & sell
some mark a pause between occasions
like a holiday a wedding
more like a game of chess
wherein the figure
holding up the queen
leans over   dies
but leaves a hole for sleep

THE GRANDMOTHERS

1

a man & a woman smiling   coming
to fulfillment in a picture
at the end of a long table with white
tablecloth   impossibly broad spoons   bread
the length of a ladder
brown & shining would delight
the grandmothers their little parched
hands holding handkerchiefs
noses fight back tears at memory of
veiled hats hidden
in the closet getting old escaping
the fond picture she grows down
to death but won't admit it
for the bride & groom

2

the oldest woman in the world kicks off
her shoes   dances on the table
she chews fat & garlic wipes bread
around the rim of plate & croaks
for water at midnight
the sleep of the grandmothers is broken
by laughter small voices from inside
the bathhouse call to her   animals invade
her bed comfortable fur
wraps around her & makes her snore
but knowing no woman will ever be clean
she blows her nose to clear it
one hand between her thighs   rinses the tight
membrane   still combs the knots out of her hair

3

past caring a grandmother
bathing checks mucus in her eyes dough
on her hands shit between
asshole & water dirt under her fingernails
her false teeth backed with gold
wax in ears snot in nose lice at pubis
still seeking to be pure the residue
of past bleedings buried with her sons
but fresh in mind she yawns from
drowsiness sometimes or belches after meals
in pain her legs feel heavy a blood spot
whirls before her   inserts a soft
white woolen cloth the cock's remembered
length inside her that returns in whiteness

4

the men by custom wait outside
her door even the young boys grandchildren
for whom the alphabet flowers in hebrew
"have respect for the body of a grandmother
"have respect for the vessel of blood
"emptied   bearer of offspring from her damp nostrils"
in the small rooms where the grandmothers
sleep they are still women
still withdrawn   glowing   in the mystery
that forbids us to drink from her cup
keeps her mattress in the center of the room
forever keeps her blood away from us
as softly the curtain flutters on her wedding night
something between a woman & a man

the idea of geometry is like the idea
of beards an idea of how the light
striking his eyeglasses makes the beards
that hang from their faces
brush the sky   a neglected dream of beards
mad Shimeon saw in their glory
sitting in a house of beards holding
the long hairs in his fist
winding & unwinding hanks of beard
oh beards I was your good shepherd once I was
the guardian of all your ringlets
king of beards & eyebrows king of armpits
beards were everywhere we turned
our hands grew beards palms bore the mouths of bearded
        women
mothers whose emblems were a goat & a baboon
who sang about beards & kingdoms old songs of home
impossible avenues forbidden towns where beards grow
hair grew in unmixed colors there was wisdom
in kisses charity spoke first from beards
but was rebuffed by strangers polacks appeared in gangs
ran us through the dawn the sun striking against Shimeon's
uplifted eyes who hoarse in praise of beards
made it to the railroad yards but perished
"oh beards I love you beards
"beards which are concealed & beards which show
"beards which begin at earline & go down
"to mouth descending & ascending covering
"the cheeks with fragrance white with ornament
"& balanced to the breastline
"beards of thirteen fountains   sources   dispositions
"first the ears
"second the corners of the mouth
"third between the nostrils
"fourth beneath the mouth from one corner to the other

18

"fifth also beneath the mouth   a tuft
"sixth ascending from below then rises to the corners fragrant
       at the upper edges
"seventh where it ends two apples grow
"eighth a tress encircling it
"ninth mingled with the eighth but braided
"tenth the tongue uncovered the hair surrounding it is lovely
"eleventh above the throat
"twelfth the fringes at its base are knotted
"thirteenth hair hanging down both sides a covering for
       the chest
besides the hair down from his shoulders pure
hippie god of light pure beard & hair
his lineage is in his face a hint of kingship
knowing no god without a beard
he curls the lowest hairs thinks about tomorrow
runs tongue around lips or presses
cool pillow to burning cheeks
a phallic beard is his but on a woman's
       face
                someone calls him
mother of the gentiles others
       are bringing lentils to his room
                still others are kissing his wet hairs
that none will be dishonored none more rich or beautiful
       than these   my strength is in my beard
                he cries my life is in it

how many would die rather than have their beards cut?

THE FATHERS

1

some were in love & grew
beautifully in the half darkness of the home
for which they lit candles
& waited still confident of business
hot for betrayals & clarity
"the vision" was its name in the old books
the title stuck only the streets
were those of a small western town in august
& some who could hardly breathe there
grew more restless still   settled
in vipertown   filled the whole country
with clothes & their dream of zion
the woman   breasts hanging down to her palms
fixed breakfast   "perfectly content to be your friend

2

the merchant with the pink thick lips
& little hanging moustache
laying tiles for you or measuring your neck
to suit you or speaking to your wife
the fat he sold you sputtering in the pan
& later   cold & white   filling a milk container
smelling of injuries & flies   was rich
but took the stagecoach regularly
to tombstone or other western towns
short of cash or pissing on the wall
back of his store   started to masturbate
a gentleman his father told him
learns to sit on air   the manners of the gentiles
haunt him   Be a brother to your wife

3

some broke through a wall   others
fatter with a smell of fish
around their lips threatened & choked
eager lovely forgetful violent
they waited at the dock
some told them it was nearly daylight
others didn't know & others
spoke of the night as though they lived in it
in love with colors some were tolerant
of sleep but nervous at remembrance
some were kings others knew kings
& dreamed about the weather
when it rained our fathers left their cities
as we were always being told

MILK & HONEY

1

Milk freezes overnight
& the skin feels it
First as a question of color & number
For reasons other than health
Or because no one else would take a chance on it
Later, having entered a home
It is easier to talk
This is your uncle, speak to him
A little
he prefers to drink milk
Says it reminds him of his wounds
& shows them
We were always close friends
Never more than that
What does it matter if his heart is good
A warm spot in my heart for him

2

Honey is practical
A device sometimes for cooling
Called honey-that-cools
Or white honey
It makes a thin line around the mouth
The color of honey matters less
But its taste is a honey taste
Always
For the man who tells you, Jews
Eat honey
You must have a ready answer
Tell him
It makes a thin line around the mouth
& tastes sweet

THE BROTHERS

to live with potatoes   not to eat them
but to live with them
they each had identical desires
& would surprise the neighbors by bellowing
if someone was good he was also
first & practical
wore long coats but kept the buttons
in his pockets   would paste
dollar bills in the pages of his books
while saying
          the music that he heard
was "really" music   how are brothers
different? everyone would ask
the world would never recognize his beauty
found him "without love but blameless"
never certain who was walking beside him
he let his daughters dream about his sons
& vanished   it was nearly Spring
but not in Poland
brothers everywhere ran through the snow
spitting, my father said
they let the ice form on their hands
but more a question of politics
than of possessions   each man made his way
badly
grew up to lose a wad of cash
brothers with faces that were always old
they tried to sleep at odd hours
one masturbated to the age of fifty
smiling   one was always telling time
a loser's life
the brother sank deeper into his own business
at night the table danced   the house
had nearly come alive
& was dangerous

there was nothing to talk about so he listened
stunned by the taste of food
a fire in his jaw   here was his father
selling gloves again
one morning he saw a rooster in the elevator
could he think of names for it?
Aladdin
Abba
Ahasuerus
every name he knew started with "a"
& pained him
now it pained him even more
he thought   the world
stopped being round or holding snow
women, slightly crazed
met him in the streets   daubed his hands
with goatshit
this was the key to paradise   the names
of paradise
were written in his heart
his brother told him
they were standing at a window crying
from their mouths
brothers have names to tell their shoes by
not their own   they were always old

A POEM FOR THE CHRISTIANS

the skull   the air   the fire
the holy name
but destitute of good works
in a land that was not sown for us
& on the sabbath day
two buicks of the previous year
without blemish
& two tenth parts of rubber
for a meal offering
mingled with gasoline
& chrome
this is the burnt offering of
every sabbath
for which rabbi yosi
left us
& rabbi abba came in his place
to praise the president
(selah)
our mouths are full of songs
(selah)
our hands hold offerings
the grieving bear   the moth
the leopard
the seven kinds of quantity & six kinds of motion
& on the sabbath day
black bodies &
bodies green with oil
& bodies gone for a burnt offering
two tenth parts for the buick
& one tenth part for the rambler
& one tenth part
for every lamb of the seven lambs
(selah)
& for their jewish god

o Shekinah o thou my defeated flower
trampled my Bessarabian daisy by the boots of strangers
cossacks have struck their cocks on thee
on thy thighs have slept generations of tartars
what bitter exiles have brought thee to this bed
to leathern blankets aflake in Polish air
contamination of lungs o my Slavic moongirl
my bride where hast thou gone then
& wherefore wherefore hast left thy milk bottles behind
thy tits will I squeeze upon for wisdom
of a milk that drops like letters
sacred alphabet soup we lap up o thou my Shekinah
do not be thus far from us in our Galician wildernesses
who scratch under our prayervests alive alive
in dream of Shekinah's entry to the tents of God
one Sabbath with not prunes to eat but grapes
would crush them on the tongue of Him
shoot colors down his beard light bursts of sex
of lightbulbs colors in the flesh of brides their marriages
to light ordained from Paradise o thou Shekinah
o daughter spread on table
with red & yellow drops thy cunt doth come undone
with drops of soul purple & black drops thy children
spring to life in thee
great is thy womb a wedding hall for saints
silken men shall dance in shall bring their beards to thee
under thy tongue shall eat in Paradise thy fat buns
& know no separation male & female
shall be one in thee
in thee the fingers of God shall come together
shall know themselves in thee o Hole o Holy Mother
o Shekinah who seeketh thy happy home around the bend
& wilt thou find it now will the memory be gone for thee
gone the forced nights in Polish brothels the whip of the
      delighted nobles

on thy ass brought low brought to thy knees in sucking homage
o cunt of God o Goddess o thou egg thou albumen
thou eye thou semen spurt thou lip thou whisper o rising into
scream
thou my SHEKINAH nerve of Elohim o soul I will split thee
now into different-colored souls
will spread thee on a white cloth under lock & key
in a cabinet inside thy father's house
then will I watch the children coming from your womb God's
keyhole
soul of Shekinah o soul of golden eels
where have I lost thee in what victory gardens hast thou gone
astray
thy feminine body shall I make a table from
in name of Aleph of the bride shall spread a white soul on
our tables
with also thy red & yellow black & purple spotted white &
soft souls
o hermaphrodite will we not bring thee balm
will wipe our essence clean upon thee
like God will cry to thee "dear child dear daughter & dear wife
"never saw a good looking woman in this world"
thou motherer o thou dear universal ass & thighs
dear light dear earth of Elohim the crown
thou hijacked innocence in flight
when will we land in what America
shall be our resting place from what cruel Polands
the angel of the exile sings above our heads & stoops
& stooping down the golden table holds you
stooping down the golden table
the song of forgotten angels in thy throat
o hymn of Shekinah on her last night from home

A Book of Testimony

THE BEADLE'S TESTIMONY

The boy who throws the ball
A jewel of a boy
His coat down to his feet
Earlocks flying

He will grow up to sell candles
Will eat a dog
& thrive on fat cigars
He will bless his mother too

Yes we are simple people
Yes we drive carts
& work with shit
Sometimes we study

Sometimes a fish in the hand
Sometimes charity
Eros is the Warsaw banker
Spain is far away

Kansas City is also far away
Where did our love go?
I have two hands & only one wallet
I want to speak to you about it

Cities & Jews
Walls & what is behind a wall
A temple sometimes
Sometimes a shining diesel locomotive

Sometimes charity
A boy's shadow on the wall
A jewel of a boy
He will grow up to sell candles

He will bless his mother too

THE STEWARD'S TESTIMONY

                        master-of-the-household
              fat old jew
called *baal* the old king's
                        name
              his fingers
blossomed in the earth dark flowers
                        covered the bannisters
              women in white kerchiefs
running to cut them loose
                        he was suffering from exhaustion
              having kicked hell out of her sides
the night before
                        his teeth had cracked against the firm white
              buttocks
crying "power" "power"
                        had tried to spread the cheeks apart
              make the double entry
in god's name
                        or by names
              hidden & lost
a man might die to know the secret of
                        he spit against the hole
              quivered
was waiting for her hand
                        to find him
              "how i do love thee, becky
"sweet rebekkah
                        "rifkeh
              "descended from a line of lublin rabbis
"rose of the dispersion
                        "yuh-buh-buh-buh-bum"
              the sight of his own penis
made him sick
                        a swollen toad
              it squatted on his belly it was

toothless
                  it puffed
         & trembled
her hand closed around it like a goose's neck
                licked its red mouth with her cowtongue
        mumbled "bridegroom"
"pig's balls"
            "little lamp of love"
      hossana!
the first busload of campers was leaving for the woods
              around him eyes
        watched from the house's open sides
schoolboys broke in
            flattened their palms against his
       ass & pressed him down
the bride
            nibbled their earlocks
      pulled the kerchiefs from their necks
beat her own head against the wall the gilded paper
          fell off in strips
     the glass case
splintered
           sending a smell of spices
      through the room the glimmer
of his riches
         silver candlesticks
   cups
candelabra
         beakers
   vases
crystal
         colored glass
     an umbrella with a silver handle
happiness
         had come to the home of
    the timber merchant
humming the eighteen benedictions
        he entered

                 numerals in ledgers fingered
his spent cock maddened
                         by his dream of a northern forest
             lumberyards
not synagogues
                     were where he worshipped
             trains run by german
engineers led to his ark
                       "the wilderness"
             the buzz of saws
to witness a new kabbala
                        whirred in his ears the young bride
             wrapped a kerchief
over his shrunken balls
                      before he stopped her
             stuffed her hole with meat
naked
                  they raced down hallways plundered
             her father's
holy relics
                   pieces of amber on which the long dead
             maggid of kozhenitz
had said prayers
                      fragments of black sugar which had touched
             the lips of the saintly
grandfather of shpoleh
                   dried herbs
             parchment
strings of wolves' teeth
                     black devil-fingers
             girdles of remnant strips
blesséd oil from the holy city of safad in the holy land
                     they smeared on their bodies
             or drank
his grey beard fell on his chest
                        a prayershawl across
             his belly
worms sang psalms from his navel the folds

                    of loose fat
              hung like dough
his penis drew back
                    & vanished
              redemption was his name for it
in our larders
                        (hidden)
              i would watch them tearing the raw
flesh they caught a calf
                    & butchered it
              smearing themselves with blood & fat
(he would drink the residue
                    called "life")
              stuck chickenfeathers to their thighs &
screamed like crows
                    not like an old man
              & his bride
the timber merchant drew heat from
                    the law
              at night he saw a mooncalf heard
distant trains
                    push toward silesia
              bought sausage from the gentiles
would drop it in the sabbath pots
                    or break into the synagogue & steal
              the prepuces of new-born infants
paradise
                    was on the road to lomza
              a tavern where the gentiles
danced for him
                    young girls opened their blouses & stood
              naked would hold their breasts up
to his lips
                    nipples the shape of acorns
              apple-colored
mushrooms between their legs
                    "how i adore defilement"
              he would cry & daub

                                                35

his phylacteries with goatshit
                    later they washed his beard
          with kvass the odors
slid into his nose
                    & made him choke
          the way home
frightened him he heard voices
                    speaking turkish
          coins rolled helplessly from his pockets
& crossed the road
                    he found the back door
          open in the pantry
skirts above her hips
                    the housemaid
          sat eyes blinded
the young bride's head moved slowly
                    in her lap a dead song
          dribbled from the timber merchant's
gums he blessed the walls but couldn't
                    find his stick
          his skullcap
fell into the soup
                    the broom had grown a mouth
          teeth he didn't know
were biting him
                    sobbing
          he learned to fly would later
become an owl
                    companion for the grandmothers in the
          "redeemed" "redeemed"   woods
the timber merchant cried
                    bandits & martyrs were dancing
          with the moon they hailed him
as their king
                    but homesick
          in his wilderness
transfigured or crushed
                    flowering or awash

               his fingers tore at his belly mangled
the folds of flesh
                    the dark wounds
          blossomed he visited
the wooded shrines around the town
                    & raged there
          would make up names
to suit himself
                    "master-of-the-household"
          "cat"
"fat face"
                    "blossomer"
          "the stump"
"the swallower of millions"

THE RABBI'S TESTIMONY

They are deceived under their hats
Because they wear them
Old men with green faces
& young men with faces growing testy

All will come at me & whisper
Rabbi, rabbi sit with us
Make our associations pleasant
For a glass of unmixed honey

How can I answer for a town of ghosts?
My lips are blue from it
Also my balls are blue
From someone's endless testimony

The rabbi will walk up & down among your women
& will pretend a birth in old age
Some days he will gamble
Others he will learn to hump among the Poles

Oh hump hump lump bump thump
The rabbi breaks his balls to save you
& is often cursed
Nightly the golden vessel bursts in two

The substance splatters
At the door called sleep he waits for you
He knows the goddess of the gentiles
But names her Sabbath

Heavy, cold, delicious, bewildered
Flowering, wounded in his nature
Not wounded really but not intact
He is not wounded or intact

But thinking: Rabbi, rabbi
Sometimes he spends his winters in Miami
These are the net benefits of love
Our fathers called disaster

THE SLAUGHTERER'S TESTIMONY

                    impeccable zeal
          of a slaughterer
his delight in the passage of generations
                    or in a bull's
          pizzle
purity of his knives
                    of all shapes & sizes
          & other commandments
with one eye closed
                    one eye open the great slaughterer
          leans across the white
washed table powerful
                    in kashrut balancing
          a drop of blood on thumbnail his kaftan
lifted high
                    spits on the black whetstone
          the green stone to polish with
white belgian stones his bookseller
                    brings him
          he dreams of small executions
animals that call him from sleep
                    pink flesh drawn tight under
          his palm
a length of gums a black lip
                    hanging loose
          skin swinging free in two directions
his fingers
                    probe the mesentery
          warts
on a goat's intestines
                    could destroy a world
          blood in milk
in eggs the blood
                    from his own gums
          weaken a slaughterer cause the sinew
of the hip to shrink from him

                              creeping things
                    to settle into the legs
of his table
                              as into flesh
                    spoiling his buckwheat
at nightfall the mothers
                              come to him
                    widows bring loaves
for the sabbath
                              the examiner beside them
                    to poke & test to ask questions
still uncertain
                              brides leave the bathhouse
                    unwashed & smelling of
his racks their blood
                              sticks to his eyelids
                    blinds him
the table & the walls turn red
                              his heart explodes against
                    his belt
buckle
                              forcing the sugar to his throat
                    red lumps
the unclean mice were carrying to their holes
                              the unclean camels
                    offered him their livers
mouthed his woolen fringes with red froth
                              red slime of slugs
                    red weasel tongues
red pelicans
                              red eyes of cormorants
                    red bats
the slaughterer falls backwards where a second
                              slaughterer
                    waits in the basement of
a synagogue he mustn't enter
                              but prays there
                    in the name of pig
with knives around his neck but

blunted caked with fat
smelling of sweat
the intruder pisses blindly puts
his own penis on
the chopping block
his balls are hairy like a lamb's
blue veins tightening with
premonitions drops of blood
red jewels
circle the cock's rim
little isaac
dances for his father the covenant
blossoms
reaches as far as poland
where crowned &
beautiful the last
empress of the gentiles
hands him his knives
shining them up with
albumen his finger
up her hole he blows
two trumpets
butchers
the maimed calf scraping
scabs from its eyes
becomes a meat god
bellows in the name of
animal & other
untasted powers of the earth
processions from the woods
that threaten him
crying
for murder of lost children in the other's
dream a slaughterer escapes
a slaughterer
splits his own skull open removing
the brain
pulling tubes from his lungs
fat & veins

from spleen then spills
milk from his stomach
hanging himself from a hook
a martyr to kashrut
he will sit at the foot of the law
in paradise
slitting the monsters' throats
will geld behemoth
throw his balls across the thousand
mountains will tie
leviathan's tongue down
with a rope
thrust a reed
through his nostrils
a thorn between his jaws
will snare the reem
that wild ox whose shit
made jordan overflow
while fearful
beneath his brows the lowest
angel helps him feed
blood to the zealous
merchants & small artisans
ranged like the letters on god's forehead
mumbling THE NAME THE NAME
in hebrew
& other holy tongues some stammering
in russian
but whose words are turned to
gold
gleaming like drops of
fat from fingers
of a slaughterer they wipe like
cherubims' on beards
eternal napkins
prayers glowing from the warming pans
where even the pious drink the blood
of angels keeping
a universe alive

42

THE STUDENT'S TESTIMONY

                    he was the last demon of ostrow
              come back to visit & play
on my mind blowing delicious
                    bubbles of red soap into
              the corners of the room
a furry singing little
                    demon with bulging eyes big
              bulging balls & all
animal twisted into shapes
                    like rubber
              "I love my demon" I would sing
& we would share the backroom of
                    the synagogue guzzling
              the gentiles' beer &
snapping paperclips
                    against the rabbi's silks reliving
              the poland of old friendships pork & fish
boiling & stinking in a single
                    pot we would dip our hands
              into & make our bellies
shine
                    what grease
              what aromas from the bookshelves
what smells of jews ripe for the sabbath
                    "fur" I would cry to him or "snot" & he
              would wrap me in his sleeves & let
their velvet warm me
                    nightly the books were opening
              in my dreams the letters
black as coal danced off
                    the page & fell on me I saw them
              cross my hips & write the double
yod upon my cock
                    "never had polish child felt
              greater warmth beside her
mother than I felt there"

later the telephone came voices
reached us from "the kingdoms"
messages of love
vibrated there were calls
from warsaw krakow moscow kiev odessa
paris berlin new york london
buenos aires hongkong yokahama bombay
melbourne juneau tombstone perth
detroit johannesburg topeka east st louis
homesick we dreamed "freedom" meaning
that our hands could touch our feet reach
even the dirt between
the toes
& breathe its essence
(of a hundred slaughterhouses
the sweet fat of the sabbath
in our teeth we waited until the women
came to us bearing the bloody eyes
of cows & lambs
they piled up on the table crying
"hossana to the gentiles")
buckwheat for dinner
in the lonely diner
eating globs of fat congealed
we played games near wealthy
homes pretending that we were children
"the luck of the jews"
"constantinople nights"
"making the devil's mark on parchment"
also "the hair & beard of macroanthropos"
through which he led me his
furry body hidden under
three suits of clothes towards other
pleasures secret holes
he lived in
bathhouse partitions white with mold
& through a broken board the eye
watched the old women strove to behold
the slit the fiery entranceway

                    dissolve
          the waters washing out the light the breath
that moves upon the waters
                              until the bulb above us splintered
          "god is one"
we sang my demon clung to me
                    made of my tongue
          his song
a master at pinochle sometimes
                    the deck flew in his hands
          beautiful men wept like children
some shelled almonds for him
                    or filled his hat with vodka
          the fat students loved him the dark ones
waited for news on the radio
                    "calm in the face of disaster"
          pilgrims visited the tsaddik's court he sat
for seven days
                    dipped figs in wine
          then lifted his milkwhite hands each
finger held a garnet
                    each eye a golden tear
          electricity ran from his beard he wore
a neon caftan
                    thrice did my demon limp into his presence
          they were face to face neither
moving neither still in love
                    or heartsick
          theirs was a meeting of the upper
& the lower worlds
                    the "model of the universe" was always
          at their call an empty building windows
broken or taped-up with X's
                    in contrast to the tsaddik's its
          easy warmth stoves in perfect order
so even a stranger had a place to sit
                    forgetful of each other
          they let the time pass with singing not
with arithmetic

                                                        45

                    "a woman for me
              & a woman for thee" (he would order)
the one with a wen near her nipple
                    the other with a glass eye women
              with moist hair in their armpits
moister below
                    & furious
              reputed to be in love with great men they were
"nieces" to all the rabbis
                    breathless my demon would mount his
              from the rear the tsaddik
slept on in innocence of
                    heart & purpose
              barely
could feel her hand
                    betray him
              but blamed it on
the tightness of his linens while
                    wan allergic dreaming
              furry to his fingers
my demon
                    slept against the other's
              side forgetting
that the bride was always chaste the sabbath
                    always an interval
              between subscriptions
something cold but beautiful
                    not a mechanical process
              merely but responsive
to the touch
                    in satin slippers beneath
              a painted canopy
of stars each waited
                    for the bride
              each called her
sabbath but each had something else a different kind of sleep
                    in mind

(coda)

                   once in a lifetime man
            may meet a hostile spirit once
he may be imprisoned for his
                   dreams & pay for them
            lightning is like oil the motor
once it starts keeps
                   running
            such was their wisdom though we had
no use for it
                   only later seeing it
            reborn
in joplin on a billboard
                   his own shadow
            was more than he could bear the war
came & he ran from it
                   back in the cellar drinking
            too much he grew thin
the great encounter ended it
                   in flames the candelabrum rose did it become
            a heart
that broke into sparks & letters
                   a shower of ruined cities from which
            my demon
vanished fled from the light when I was born

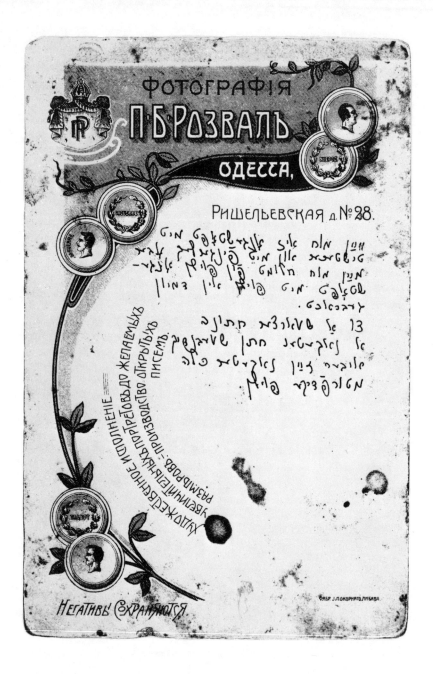

A Book of Writings

ANCESTRAL SCENES (I)

old crystal   a dry
piece of cake
remains
on the plate

        also herring scraps
        radishes
        slice of blackbread
        tea-leaves
        etc.

  the man who farts
  likes it
  letting his muscles relax

  & feels inky
  more like a sponge than a man

how alarming, how
vulgar
they said, their way
of speaking

said it

ANCESTRAL SCENES (II)

                    my grandfather's death
          was foolish
he wiped his ass with
                  dirty newsprint
          died of blood poisoning in 1914
had been a merchant
                  stationery
          wire thimbles
glass beads
                  brooches
          "notions"
a tray of cotton spools
                  he would find a chair
          piled high with
cushions
                  broken springs
          where he could sleep
dying
                  would dream of
          selling lemons
yellow notebooks
                  the little
          stinking ends of jewish
vursht

ANCESTRAL SCENES (III)

a small golden
snuffbox

> otherwise
> rabbinic collar
> but open at the throat

> a young man's beard
> offsets
> an old man's face

the first
electric bulb
lies splintered

"on a morning before the first world war
    electricity brought us lights"

mitzraim was only another name for egypt

> salt in your eyes!
> pepper in your nose!

ANCESTRAL SCENES (IV)

young boy standing on
a table
from his clothes hang
watches   jewelry
saffron-lidded eyes of his old grandfather
stare into his
between them start
processions of
pale jewish angels
throwing coins
that roll against the icing
of a cake
into which dough is traced
words of power
the picture of a fish
& many small holes
punched
into the surface
"therefore they called this cake a sieve"

AMULET

"Joseph
"is a fruitful bough
"a fruitful
"bough by eye of

"water
"branches who run over
"wall
"a wall runs

"over
"branches
"on the eye
"upon

A POLISH ANECDOTE   1931

"snuff too weak" you
soak in whiskey
you mix with fine pepper
your nose grows warm
& fat from it
you become a wealthy man
by sneezing
everybody says "god bless you"
the hairs inside your nose
grow hairs

A POLISH ANECDOTE   "Victory"

"he died among colleagues" runs
the Polish epitaph   the body
falls down from the saddle without
sorrow & the other soldiers

ride their horses over him singing
"sleep sleep dear colleague
"in your dark grave
"we wish you sweet dreams about Poland"

beautiful losses etc where each man
has many colleagues only one friend
said Marshal Pilsudski   "to be vanquished &
not to surrender   this is victory!"

A POLISH ANECDOTE   "The Saint"

the man who wouldn't kill an insect
scratched his balls
all day & half the night
would have the rabbi bless his pockets
smiled but never
at a woman   wouldn't even face his wife
but stared out the window
hands behind back he always placed
one foot before the other
remembering the saint who didn't know
his own wife had a wooden leg
until they buried her

A POLISH ANECDOTE   "The Banquet"

four serving spoons
in one dish of
fermented rye

barscz what greater
treat than this for
you   my children?

in a heavy
bowl or crock com-
bine flour &

boiling water
to a thick dough
let stand loosely

covered in a
warm spot in the
kitchen for at

least forty-eight
hours when the
dough begins to

rise add a quart
of cold water
let stand until

the liquid is
completely clear
to use remove

liquid without
stirring discard
when the dough be-

comes too slimey

she missed her period
hysteria
the rabbi said
& knew it!

wisemen generations
of sages
have walked before us
not tightlipped

not bachelors & fruitless
but wisemen!
could look at a woman
& say

she missed her period?
hysteria
the mole over her lip
a sign of grace

A POLISH ANECDOTE   "The Noble"

getting dead drunk he bled his jewish
barber with a shaky hand
or hiding from the cossacks still shouted
to the man who hid him
"take off your cap you jewish cunt"
a Radziwill can keep a boy's face
in a pail of water can make him
drink & puke then laugh at their women
forced to sit in trees crowing like
cocks would shower them with bullets
watch them fall & run but always
throw them coins or kiss another
Radziwill while mumbling
"beloved brother   go to hell!"

AMULET

"Black Striga
            black on black
"who eats black blood
                    & drinks it
"like an ox she bellows
"like a bear she growls
"like a wolf she crushes

THE NEOLITHIC DREAM OF RABBI NACHMAN

for Gary Snyder

a Jew so mad he heard the flowers
in the woods   singing
& understood each word
"them ice plants would've blowed your mind"

(says Rabbi Nachman) growing old
once slept inside a house
made of young trees   in dreams
he walked with the dead

& told his landlord
"you have killed these souls
"before their time
"but said no prayer for them

a poem for Rabbi Snyder

MORE VISIONS FROM THE NEOLITHIC RABBIS

for Nathaniel Tarn

first a steambath
then the men dived into
a muddy pool

water that smelled of
gasoline & sulphur
like all the pools in Beltz

that night they sang
"sweet love
"approach

"sweet love your bride
"is here
"o Bride o Sabbath Queen

& walked outside   saw
stars of Ukraine
were fat like oranges

a poem for Rabbi Tarn

A POEM FROM THE SAINT'S LIFE

his father called him a little flame
no no he was a blazing fire
he brought two mountaintops together
would carry a castle from the east
& set it in the king's yard
dreamy servants walked round the walls
bothered by the climate
they would confuse the meat & cheese
his dogs spoke hebrew   even
the birds wore prayershawls carried
rings in beaks
the names of God engraved in
amethyst   how tall
the saint grew
he started walking on a Friday
from Lodz to Mazowietz
managed to get there by the evening meal

AMULET

pishon	gihon	hiddekel	euphrates
nohsip	nohig	lekeddih	setarhpue
euphrates	hiddekel	gihon	pishon
setarhpue	lekeddih	nohig	nohsip
hiddekel	gihon	pishon	euphrates
lekeddih	nohig	nohsip	setarhpue
pishon	hiddekel	gihon	euphrates
nohsip	lekeddih	nohig	setarhpue

The rivers of Paradise

From THE CODE OF JEWISH LAW

1

the worm because it
creeps you may not
eat of it   therefore

they threw out vinegar
& fruit they threw out
cereals or sifted them

with fish they searched
brains   intestines   liver
mouth & ears

round as a lentil were
those worms
some on their bodies

by their fins some
in their mouths
others beneath the gills

2

THE LOVERS

desired a partition
40″ high

to block the light
not even moonlight

lit her body
lamplight

from another room
they shut out

with her fallen dress
& in the dark

wouldn't look between her legs
or kiss that place

in hunger
"to make yourselves detestable"

3

to let a rooster
wander

with a thread tied
to one leg

preventing it from
breaking dishes

but broke the law of rest
on saturdays

4

THE PROHIBITIONS

sowing   plowing   reaping   sheaving   threshing   winnowing
cleansing crops   grinding   sifting   kneading   baking
shearing   blanching   carding   dyeing   spinning   weaving
making a minimum of two loops   weaving two threads   sep-
arating two threads   tying   untying   sewing a min-
imum of two stitches   ripping out in order to sew them
hunting a gazelle   slaughtering it   flaying it   salting

it   curing scraping or slicing its hide   writing a
minimum of two characters   erasing in order to write
them   building   wrecking   extinguishing   kindling
hammering   transporting

        & did not walk out with
        a needle   but only with a pin
        for clothes
        a watch became a burden
        though a silver key was more
        for show & eyeglasses
        wouldn't be carried not even
        in a silver frame
        "add no cloth to clothing for
        "the rain (they said)
        "unless against discomfort
        "a cane for lameness
        "but on the sabbath
        "the lame & the blind stay inside
        "with the chained man
        "others knowing that it's wrong to
        "walk on stilts through mud
        "& water right
        "to wear a bandage of
        "poor cloth
        "& go out with cotton in your ear
        "or cotton wads against
        "a woman's
        "bleeding   not to
        "spare her clothes but
        "give her comfort
        "a man may wear two coats if one
        "is for a friend
        "likewise two pairs of slippers
        "two hats
        "two belts   also (they said)
        "avoid a rope with two
        "knots in it to hold
        "your pants up   take off all

"suspenders
"& put no handkerchief
"around thy neck
"or leg
"no gloves on hands
"but wear
"a toupee on thy head
"of flax or wool
"the woman who holds
"an eagle-stone
"against miscarriage may
"still walk freely
"on the sabbath

5

circumcision
at a graveside

they give the child
a name

but pronounce no
benediction

to cut off
that disgrace

6

don't eat the blood
in eggs   (she said)
the blood in fish wd satisfy her
but don't serve it gathered
in a vessel fearing
people wd talk she also feared
biting a crust of break wd crack
her gums & draw blood in

she wd later cut away   wd watch
for blood in milk
particles of meat between her teeth
of cheese on table she ate meat from
rinsed her mouth   swept her tablecloth
& baking goat in milk-of-almonds
wd put whole almonds in
fearing people wd see the whiteness & wd talk

7

going from darkness to
a well-lit room
opened the door a crack

looked at a little light
then eased it further
& walked in

because the sun is gradual
he was   & feared it
in reflection

wdn't have windows facing north
even so wanted
a sky without obstructions

didn't read at dusk but not
at midday either
avoided staring at anything

too white   but red
cd hurt him also   smoke could
or fine dust against his eyes

sulphurous odors
strong wind blowing in his face
excessive breathing   tears

68

"my eyes do fail with tears"
but more with too much fucking
"the precept of the lord is pure

"enlightening the eyes"

8

a dangerous proposition   fish
& meat together
even if it's chickenfat
but water
between courses helps
wash the food down   rinse the mouth
& sweat a problem
too   a poison
really   not the face's
sweat I mean the body's therefore
he never put food
under his clothes he never
bit coins that sweat
had clung to   he was very clean
if spit formed in his mouth
while smelling food
he never swallowed it avoiding
danger to his body

9

THE ENCHANTMENTS

he said the bread dropped from his mouth
the cane fell from his hand
his son called him from behind

a raven croaked at him
a deer crossed his path
a snake passed on his right

a fox passed on his left
& ruined his journey
as a bird's singing might

he said he couldn't pay
it was too early
he said it was the sabbath

the new moon frightened him he said
the hen should die for crowing
like a cock & meant: the hen should die

10

your hands are full of blood
because you think of it
& touch it
you make it hard by
sleeping on it
or leaning up against a friend
or watching animals & birds die
even by riding horseback
or holding it while pissing
or soaping it
or wearing your pants too tight
or reading books by gentiles
or eating fatty foods
or by not eating fatty foods
but turning over in your sleep
& farting in a cold bed
the milk from your own body
running down your leg
staining the sheets with dishonor
yellow & stiff
by morning
that has made you a murderer
someday will raise
the midnight lament for

the temple   demanding
repentance to hold
the circumcised babe by its leg
smile at the iron-toothed mother
but turn from the shame of
your flesh   in love
& the pursuit of peace

AMULET

master	occupied	sang	under
of	shadows	drove	ritual
dreams	the	breath	fringes
led	moon	further	like
his	dancers	down	letters
party	trembled	it	his
marched	beautiful	emerged	name
to	men	in	shapes
volhynian	lifted	red	22
woods	gowns	cloud	verbs

TREE SPIRIT EVENTS (Zohar)

Then sing the trees of the wood for joy
before the Lord.

One mounts to one side.
One descends on that side.
One enters between the two.
Two crown themselves with a third.
Three enter into one.
One produces various colors.
Six of them descend on one side & six of them on the other.
Six enter into twelve.
Twelve bestir themselves to form twenty-two.
Six are comprised in ten.
Ten are fixed in one.

ALPHABET EVENT (1)

Recite the 221 alphabets while walking in a circle.
Repeat the event 442 times.

ALPHABET EVENT (2)

Do the first Alphabet Event walking backwards.
Recite the alphabets starting from the end.

And I walked by his side & he took me by his hand &
raised me upon his wings & showed me those letters, all of
them, that are graven with a flaming sword on the throne of
glory: And sparks go forth from them & cover all the chambers
of 'Araboth.

WORD EVENT

He sits in a house whose walls are decorated with fresh
vegetables, praying & singing psalms, & reading from *The
Book of Law.*
Then he begins to move the letters that he sees, until they
make new words & sounds.
Quickly he jumps from word to word, letting the words
form thoughts in any order.
Finally he drops the words out of his mind: word by word
until he thinks of nothing.
Freed from thought, the consonants dance around him in
quick motion. Forming a mirror in which he sees his face.

BOOK EVENT

Bring an old book to a cemetery & bury it.

WOMAN'S EVENT (1)

A woman washes face & hands in water mixed with the sap of an apple tree.

WOMAN'S EVENT (2)

At the foot of a fruit tree a woman buries a bowl filled with menstrual blood.

WOMAN'S EVENT (3)

A woman crawls under the belly of a pregnant mare.

WOMAN'S EVENT (4)

A woman strokes the limbs of a bride or bridegroom.

WOMAN'S EVENT (5)

A woman drinks a mixture of wild tea leaves, or a woman eats a rooster complete with comb & gizzard, or a woman drinks water seeped in the ashes of a burnt male rabbit.

WOMAN'S EVENT (6)

A woman swallows the foreskin of a newly circumcised infant.

THE NUMBERS (1)

Then did the Master read the text: All sevens are beloved.

Then he said: Take seven prickles from seven palm trees, seven chips from seven beams, seven nails from seven bridges, seven ashes from seven ovens, seven scoops of earth from seven door-sockets, seven pieces of pitch from seven ships, seven handfuls of cumin, & seven hairs from the beard of an old dog, & tie them to the neckhole of the shirt with a white twisted cord.

And Again:
4 lamps
4 ladders
4 children of the flowers of the priesthood
shook 4 willow branches
toward the 4 directions

THE NUMBERS (2)

She wears
pearls.
Makes a bag of black velvet
for her husband
& a gold star.
She adds honey to his milk.
He asks for raisins
& cherry juice.
His coat is made of fox fur.
Barefoot
they go running.
Seven.

Seven.
Seven.
Seven.
Seven.
Four.

She waves a goosewing
duster.
They drink brandy from tin mugs.
Carp's head
wrapped in cabbage leaves
for dinner.
He buys a strip of licorice from a Turk.
She wears a beaded jacket.
He smokes a long pipe with an amber mouthpiece.
She smokes sweet-smelling cigarettes.
Seven.

Seven.
Seven.
Seven.
Seven.
Four.

Her shoes are pointed.
His shoes are sometimes made of straw.
Sometimes he drinks from a red-painted glass.
She washes her breasts with rainwater.
Four.

Four.
Four.
Four.
Four.
Four.
Four.
Four.
Seven.

He wears a thirteen-pointed hat
edged with skunk.
The letters he draws look like mountains.
His wife writes Hebrew like a man.
He makes her repeat the names of angels.
Four.

Four.
Four.
Four.
Four.
Four.
Four.
Four.
Seven.

She pulls the longboots
off his feet.
The sound of gramophones
comes through their windows.
She walks on her hands.
He taps on her shutters with
his wooden hammer.
His chairs turn over
his dishes break.
Later he stops the clock.
Her eyes are different
colors.
Seven.

Seven.
Seven.
Seven.
Seven.
Four.

He carries a snuffbox made of bone.
A silver pouch holds his tobacco.

She chews on a coin with her gold teeth.
He tells her to let the boiled milk form a skin.
Four.

Four.
Four.
Four.
Four.
Four.
Four.
Four.
Seven.

Hot peppered peas under
a mass of rags.
Squab & egg noodles for dinner.
His pitchblack beard with its two points.
Cow bladders in place of
windows.
Hands in a tub of yellow dough.
A trace of hair on the Queen's feet.
The smile of a man who speaks pure German.
Seven.

Seven.
Seven.
Seven.
Seven.
Four.

"SHE"

1

She Shekinah
She Kingship
She Dwelling

She Daughter
She Lady
She Pearl

She Precious
She Cornerstone
She Female

She Floweth
She Male
She Garden

She Garment
She Earth
She Ocean

She Omen
She Lady of Light
She Sarah

She Slave
She Sucketh the Gods
She Rebekkah

She Rachel
She Leah
She Moon with the Hair

She the Hoverer

2

She Matronit
She Dancer
She Northerner

She in the Night
She Agrath
She Igrath

She Ishtar
She Tail of the Comet
She Child

She Charmer
She Crooked
She Serpent

She Stiff Necked
She Stick
She Lilith

She Liar
She Thorn
She Screech Owl

She Stranger
She Alien Crown
She Heaven

She Howler
She Hole
She the Hole for the Dead

She Dazzler

AMULET

אבג יתץ קרע שטן נגד יכש בטר צתג...
ל סזק שקוצית בשכמלו בשם שדי יוי
לילית
אביטי אביזו
אמרוסו הקש אודם
איק סודו אייל ומטרוסה
אבגו קטה שטרוגה קלי
בטוח חיל י סריט
טהש

Galician Nights, or A Novel in Progress

GALICIAN NIGHTS, OR A NOVEL IN PROGRESS

The Early Life, Loves & Circumstances of Esther K.

1

Because a Jew eats meat & grows fat he waits until he sees the Governor.

The Jew's beard is sleek, so are his eyes sleek & shameless in an otherwise bland face.

Greetings, says Jew to Governor, but the Governor doesn't respond, no he stands there smiling.

At once the Jew gives him a fat portion & draws back.

Ah, says the Governor in awe. His fingers dip into the dish, dip & are lost.

Does the Jew withdraw then?

No.

Does the Governor return to purge his land of Jews?

No the Governor doesn't return nor does he purge his land.

What does he do then?

He trembles on the balance of a kiss, he dawdles, he grows sick, he waves his arms, he vanishes, he is heard of nevermore.

2

He trembles on the balance of a kiss, he dawdles, he grows sick, he waves his arms, he vanishes, he is heard of nevermore.

The Governor is lost, she says, says it & goes inside the house.

The cart standing in her studio is the same one they rode around the town.

My love! cries Esther K. as she undresses.

Sometimes he rushes from her room, naked himself & with a sock around his forehead.

Reddish eyelids, yellow melancholy eyes, he was her gentile, she called him "little goy."

Now she puts snuff in both her nostrils.

It is evening. It is 1931 in Poland. It is better to be naked. It is more than that. It is worth it. Is it? It is too soon. It is noon. It is like early November it is really June.

And Esther K. is bathing.

Greet the Governor for me, winks Esther K., & rubs the soap between her thighs.

Her gold tooth glitters.

The mirror swings along its golden chain. He is dreaming again of gold utensils.

A little to the left, a little shy, a little heavy in his socks, a little wet, a little like her father, a little less, a little lonely

if you sneeze, he says & turns aside.

I love you.

What a dove is Esther K.!

3

And what a dove is born to Esther K.!

Greetings remarketh the Governor.

They have come in procession to bless the child of her flesh, the midwife removeth it as one removeth a thorn.

A white-haired child which smelleth of old laundry.

Soon Esther K. ariseth from her bed red ribbons around her leg & bangeth the door shut.

(This was in fulfillment of her dream.)

She cutteth the navel string & putteth a grain of salt beneath the infant's tongue. She rubbeth white honey upon her lips, also upon his arms.

They drop a honeycomb into his cradle.

Will Esther K. see the produce of her womb beyond this morning?

Perhaps so perhaps no, says Esther K. & sings *O little golden one sleep in thy cradle,* her own first song.

Galician nights, how beautiful & how lonely

but for the Jewess who has tasted of the Gentiles' honey there is no reunion in her father's tent

no awning of white satin no wedding knives no tribal

beard to hide her face beneath.

O Esther K. thou my semitic beauty thou easter excellence
thou poor foresaken witness yet plyest thy trade in peace!

Thou warmest a towel for the Governor.

Thou wearest a rose gown.

(A man, once come on business, learneth to stay & bathe
with thee.)

Thou eatest tripe & poppy seeds.

Thou sharest half thy bounty with the rich.

4

Esther K. receives a letter from China. It reads:

Darling Esther K.

This is a wonderful Chinese city & there is here also a
wonderful Jewish community. The center of the life of the
community is its remarkable synagogue which is reputed to be
very ancient. The community itself is said also to be very
ancient & to go perhaps back to the lost tribe of Asher, one of
the famous ten lost tribes of Israel. Isaiah the Prophet speaks
of Jews who had settled in the land of the Sinim, but be that
as it may it is certain that from the 7th century on, Persian
Jews were coming into China by way of India. There are today
four thousand Jews in China whose appearance is not to be
distinguished from that of the Chinese. But don't let that
fool you since they all play Mah Jong according to the Ash-
kenazic variation so familiar to us & not the rather simpler
native form. There is also in the city a good theater, several
western-style beauty parlors & at least one kosher restaurant
managed by a family of Russian exiles. Charity abounds here.
The Sisterhood flourishes. The study of the Law, while not
brilliant, is steady, & at least it imposes few new burdens. The
climate is "ideal."

In addition a wonderful man resides here whom you would
love to meet. While I cannot divulge his name I am at liberty
to inform you that his initials are L.L. A trip to this corner of
the Diaspora will truly change your life.

(N.B. When you have finished reading this letter make six copies & sign your name to each, then remit them to six of your dearest friends. You must do this within three days of receipt or disastrous consequences will follow; if you comply however the results will bring you instantaneous good luck. (Holofernes failed to comply & was beheaded by Judith: Count Potocki complied & was spared to meet God as a martyr.))

It is a serious matter, dearest, & a sure sign of the coming triumph of the Lord's Anointed!

The letter bears a lion in the lower corner
& a sacred lemon.
There is otherwise no signature.

5

Circumstances in a Jewish house.

Circumstances of Esther K.

Circumstances of men exchanging wallets in front of the guildhall.

Circumstances of carts circumstances of leather lines in the hands of the master drivers.

Circumstances of farewells. Of parades of gymnasts on the road to Warsaw.

Circumstances of Bialystok & what lay beyond.

Circumstances of buttons circumstances of sewing each thread into place not leaving the ends untied.

Circumstances of half understood lines in three rhyming poems by distinctively different Yiddish poets.

Circumstances in a Jewish house.

Circumstances of "gypsy costumes & Polish happenings in the woods."

Circumstances of chance meetings in the market.

Gentile circumstances & circumstances filled with danger.

Circumstances of letters written under cover of night.

Circumstances of the beautiful rape.

(Some circumstances that were easy others that brought great riches.

Circumstances & insurance.)

Circumstances of Esther K.

Circumstances of the journey Esther K. took across the ocean.

Circumstances of her noble station on Attorney Street.

Circumstances of the queen among the Persians the Governor is kind to her she bites his beard.

Circumstances of the 7:10 to Warsaw & the 8:35 to Babylon.

Circumstances of better times when will we come on better times again?

Circumstances of Esther K. & China.

Circumstances of Jews in pigtails & of a visit by the false messiah Leo Levy.

Circumstances of his dream of Shabtai Tswi's dream of a Turkish heaven.

Circumstances of the Shekinah leaning on his arm.

Circumstances of the Shekinah with twelve breasts & of her lover with only two hands to caress them.

Circumstances of the Shekinah in a sea of milk.

Circumstances of her return to Poland.

(O Poland of the saints unbuttoned Poland repeating endlessly the triple names of Mary.)

Circumstances of King Casimir & the Jewish queen who sat beside him.

Circumstances of a Kazar kingdom ruled by women.

Circumstances of a golden foreskin.

Circumstances of the monarch strangled by a silky rope then buried in Paradise with forty others.

Circumstances of the legends I never knew that were kept from me in childhood.

Circumstances of her mind & ours.

Circumstances of her own face appearing in the Polish rotogravure (a decade later in the Denver Post).

Circumstances of smoked mackerel.

Circumstances of her mother's hands around a goose's neck. Of hers around the fatmeat of the King of Poland.

Circumstances of heaven circumstances of halvah circumstances of half a loaf.

(I have brought you these circumstances toward a tale of Esther K.)

Circumstances of Galician nights circumstances on the road to Warsaw & on Attorney Street.

Circumstances in Persia China & the Kazar Kingdom.

Circumstances of the cost of milk & honey.

Circumstances in a Jewish house.

Circumstances of the loves of Esther K.

A Morning in the Life of Mister Leo Levy

1

He went to sleep in Jewishtown woke up early the next morning feeling how forlorn it was to be lost & foundering from three directions.

The demon was gone, gone too the bench but not misst.

(His own was too long for comfort.)

(Too much of a secret.)

He waked between rooms a separate landscape coming to life in each hand.

Elijah!

As his name beckoned his eye would surge past extremi-

ties the remembered morning's socks buried in each boot he
had to dig his hand into & couldn't bear it.

He sighed then, one short *oy* for each long *vey* & several
ays (eyes) (I's) along the edges, let them hear him if they
minded or touch the pasty cloth in place of.

Pheh.

The leather had natural holes to it washed by several
months of russias snowfalls polands muds pebbled water by
the black sea pricked by thorns of bukavina dungedup roads
of hungary sizzledover fires drafty synagogues were-full-of
scorched & cracked like holy relics.

(Oy!)

So saying he has turned himself away his legs drawn in
against his chest (he coughs & makes them tremble) in a rage
with life.

2

But his longcoat (black) was on a large chair (yellow) in
which a lion (red) was carved, the letters *lamed beth yod hey*
above it like his own name Leo Levy not the name he used in
his profession but reminded of it always anyhow when seeing
that symbol of old powers the exile kept alive.

A lion by birth a liar later, hah!

He hated tea less than he loved money so had to be stuck
with the taste of it.

A lemon.

The pulp had turned brown with the night's passing,
more dirt & corruption to contend with. Brown of piss in pot.
Why had he brought his powers to this place. A pox no a
cholera on it!

Contagion.

This comes from being a jew.

The doctors (victims themselves) had no name for it.

One, who was preeminent among his fellows, came to the
house (it was the week of tabernacles) & prescribed immediate
retirement.

His health was dependent on it, his home so far away. The doctor had to be brought into his confidence (& was!) before there was any hope for a return to his senses.

Why blackbread? he was asked.

Why onions?

Why break the bread into small pieces & cut the onion rings with the middle fingernail & thumbnail?

He had been going at it wrong & had made himself sicker.

There was little hope now.

Less for those who sat around him in the bathhouse.

Would he tell them beautiful stories of his youth in Fairbanks?

Yes he had the fingers of a jeweler.

Yes one eye was blue.

3

The other eye was impossible to know any longer, though one would guess it the same color as its still present member.

Yet since nothing is certain (thus was it written in the Talmud where it was also written that everything would be known) you could hardly argue from the glass back to the jelly.

The glass was green.

Sovereign pickles floated in a tub of brine, they were the first sight after his long surgery

mirrored in the green eye too they trembled in the blue one like the gnarled moist fingers of a manyhanded idol.

Will she recognize me when we meet again or I her now that the world is flattened in my sight?

Her buxomness, her boobs I frankly sucked, her plums her bosoms her delights her apertures her jellied (gelid) roundness.

Flat? *Drat!*

He rips it from its socket then hurls it with a *zets* against the wall.

Oy what a carnage was what lamentations were.
This is the angry song that Leo Levy made for Esther K.:

Angry Song

I hate Esther K. because I am ugly

I hate Esther K. & am angry at her because I am ugly

I hate Esther K. & am angry at her contempt for me because I
am ugly

I hate Esther K. & am angry at her contempt for me which I
deserve less than she knows because I am ugly

I hate Esther K. & am angry at her contempt for me which I
deserve less than she knows being estranged from me be-
cause I am ugly

I hate Esther K. & am angry at her contempt for me which I
deserve less than she knows being estranged from me who
went to sleep in Jewishtown because I am ugly

I hate Esther K. & am angry at her contempt for me which I
deserve less than she knows being estranged from me who
went to sleep in Jewishtown I feel so sad because I am
ugly

I hate Esther K. & am angry at her contempt for me which I
deserve less than she knows being estranged from me who
went to sleep in Jewishtown I feel so sad to be a forni-
cator of demons because I am ugly

I hate Esther K. & am angry at her contempt for me which I
deserve less than she knows being estranged from me who
went to sleep in Jewishtown I feel so sad to be a forni-
cator of demons & to smell of onions because I am ugly

I hate Esther K. & am angry at her contempt for me which I
deserve less than she knows being estranged from me who
went to sleep in Jewishtown I feel so sad to be a forni-
cator of demons & to smell of onions & to see God's pickles
with my true blue eye because I am ugly

I hate Esther K. & am angry at her contempt for me which I
deserve less than she knows being estranged from me who
went to sleep in Jewishtown I feel so sad to be a forni-

cator of demons & to smell of onions & to see God's pickles
with my true blue eye & nothing with my lovely glass eye
because I am ugly

I hate Esther K. & am angry at her contempt for me which I
deserve less than she knows being estranged from me who
went to sleep in Jewishtown I feel so sad to be a forni-
cator of demons & to smell of onions & to see God's pickles
with my true blue eye & nothing with my lovely glass eye
no this is no way to treat the Lord's anointed because I
am ugly

OY OY OY IT'S HARD TO BE A JEW!

THE SEVEN MELODIES OF ESTHER K.

1

The pink head of her father
under a black skullcap.
Radishes.

2

Will you visit us up the stairs.
(I had climbed there already.)
We sat in a circle of worshippers.
He said   My name is Leo Levy.
(I loved the name.)
& his hair reached down to his shoulders.
Comb it comb it
he cried.
(I took the comb &
jammed it down.
Electricity ran from his beard.)

3

Did Jews learn to smile?
they asked him.
His answer was "once"
"maybe" came easy to his lips
it was a way
of smiling   serious   amused
& with a smile.

4

A marriage to the Jewish king.
& a Chinese holiday.
Good fortune.
Clear sailing.
Bright days.
Happiness is just around the corner.

5

Ride on my white leopard.
(Give me a boost.)
He said yes.
(Can I stand on your shoulders.)
Only if you promise not to fall.
(I do.)
There's Jerusalem.
(You can't come into Jerusalem on a leopard.)
Then on what.
(A rickshaw pulled by goats.)
No a chariot.
(Then a chariot pulled by leopards.)
No by donkeys.
(You can't come into Jerusalem on a donkey.)

6

In love with a gypsy
how beautiful
my days are   my feet
begin in Vilna
& carry me to Havana.
He rubs my pudenda
& buys me a manicure.
I will follow his motorcycle
up the Great Wall of China.

7

Two hundred & forty-eight parts of her body.
Three hundred & sixty-five veins.

VARIATION ON A JEWISH LOVE SONG

(The Sixth Melody of Esther K.)

In love with a gypsy
how beautiful
my days are   my feet
begin in Vilna
& carry me to Havana.
He rubs my pudenda
& stuffs it with his frankfurter.
I will follow his motorcycle
up the Great Wall of China.

ISAAC LURIA'S "HYMN TO SHEKINAH FOR THE FEAST OF THE SABBATH" NEWLY SET ROSH HASHONAH 5733 BY JEROME ROTHENBERG

I have sung
an old measure

would open
gates to

her field of apples
(each one a power)

set a new table
to feed her

& beautifully
candelabrum

drops its
light on us

Between right & left
the Bride

draws near in
holy jewels

clothes of the sabbath
whose lover

embraces her
down to foundation

gives pleasure
squeezes his strength out

in surcease of
sorrow

& makes new faces
be hers

& new souls
new breath

gives her joy
double measure

of lights & of
streams for her blessing

o Friends of the Bride
go forth

give her many
sweet foods to taste

many kinds of
fish

for fertility
birth

of new souls
new spirits

will follow the 32 paths
& 3 branches

the bride with
70 crowns

with her King who
hovers above her

crown above crown in
Holy of Holies

this lady all worlds are
formed in

all's sealed
within her

shines out from
Ancient of Days

Toward the south
I placed

candelabrum
(o mystical)

room in
the north

for table
for bread

for pitchers of wine
for sweet myrtle

gives power to
lovers

new potencies
garlands

of words for her
70 crowns

50 gates
the Shekinah

ringed by
6 loaves

of the sabbath
& bound

all sides to
Heavenly Refuge

the hostile
powers

have left us
demons you feared

sleep in chains

Esther K. Comes to America

a gallery of Jews, love
so perfect it becomes
a solid thing   a person's
or a monster's face made of candles
"if we could only hold the lips
in place" the pink flesh
falls   how beautiful & old
(the women sing) this is no graven image
it is the body of your father
sleeping he was young
he would only wake up to read a book
or smell the rolls
baking in the oven his sisters
cared for
others were walking
in the woods still others
had vanished among the Gentiles
young girls in neckties
riding horses some would buy
magazines with pictures of Polish cities
some wrote to Paris or U.S.A.
& wouldn't eat
Sundays were spent in groups
girls held each other
but spoke of lovers
from the towns   even the young men
sitting on each other's laps
dreamed freedom
on distant walls the wax
was running down
like tears their mothers
wept on Fridays
while waiting for the meat & prunes
still in love
the sisters fitted neatly

into the picture of the perfect town
the young men left for Cuba
farewells
not blessings followed
where they went
the sun was always going down
& shifted
one made a movie   he would dance
his way through life
forgetting his mother's baldness
the virtues that made a woman strong
he fell in love with Gentiles
real blondes were always on his lawn
speaking in German
he would strip down & ride them
psalms burst from his throat
"honkeytonk joys" delivered in a mock accent
he flew westward
to California   no one
wore corsets now
though some forgot how to smile
others would praise him for his teeth
his eyes were ageless
like his clothes
only the pockets changed
the papers faded
walking on country roads at night
still holding hands
the women kept heading toward the towns
old friends had died
along the way to   she could tell you
the exact location of each grave
minutes added up
they would be charged for them in dollars
growing poorer
someone would shuffle the cards
but no one was playing
the photos had slipped into her lap

her glasses fogged
the miracle was that the candle
could keep burning
that there was no one
holding it above his head
to let the wax drip down
the wax had gathered in a metal dish
yellow & pink it sputtered
in the candle's light

THE IMMIGRANT

for Charles Chaplin

feathers hang from the fingers of the immigrant
who will embrace an egg   whose eyelids
even now close over the first half-dollar in the world
a moon for the desert America was building
suddenly gone haywire falling soft & cheezey
down an endless line of streets with restaurants
polished floors you slid on as the waiter
the electrician sometimes even sometimes
the man who finds a stranger's wallet
in his soup   runs off from there
to yellowstone poor epileptic honeymooner
who wears a bearcoat in the Rockies
your bear-love licking at your trail
far from Newark desperado with a rubber gun
you make your final shootout with the bearded lawmen
but earlier the week you rode in steerage
Rotterdam receded only the smell of sausages
brought Poland back that and the message
of the unwashed cunt the lady in the bunk above you
aimed at your nose bright sexual pickles

a garlic polka with all the words changed into Yiddish
the Hungarian tenor intercepted slipping
a hand into her drawers then left you
seated on a stoop in Monroe Street an orphan
unattentive to the band that played The Immigrant Shuffle
you learned to labor slowly
at first but tested your dreams of leisure
in the bitter factories the dark Jew
was your boss the bright Jewess
worked beside you on the line
would fill your dinnerpail with stuffed dough
chickpeas incredible farmer cheeses wrapped in rags
tastes that lit up names in your mind
from the old town   of girls with poppyseed eyes
smiles of white raisins
whose mouths still moist from puddings
encircled your putz their heavy
honeydew breasts cut open licked clean
later in your secular imagination
sleeping with the German collie you attempted
abominations to the rabbis hugged the gentle fur
in friendship your first drop of semen
freed you   maddened   into cabarets
to sing the song scrawled on your shirtsleeve
the words in middle European ageless anthem of your race
no demoralized proletarian you were
the sweet soul in exile cockeyed scholar
who couldn't spell his name but stood
three hours in long underwear (torn in back to show
a handsome pair of balls) outside the steamroom
devised a fancy maneuver to keep a step
ahead of the Sicilian faggot with raised bathbrush
twirling his heavy moustaches soaked in pepper
gaily you put your lips to his then sneezed him
through the doorway   falling   saw his cruel life
snuffed under the feet of marchers
strikers you led down East Street & up into Heaven
became an Irish cop yourself but kept your earlocks

your gaberdines hidden you still ate radishes for lunch
scraps of chickenwings for dinner let the skin
slide down your throat & choke you
the contradictions were almost a relief
for some for you the clock kept spinning
wheels hummed in the tower
everything ran by electricity & worried you
nickels & dimes sparked into life they bounced
off counters into your cuffs now you were always bending
looking at your shoes would even stick chewing gum
on broomsticks sought lost gold down manholes
from there you took the steamer
to Alaska trudged endless miles from Fairbanks
with your Yukon love   howling   you wore a derby
suspenders pulled your pants up to your chest
& left you gasping   visions from last year's snowstorms
filled your eyes & mind with gold
gold were your watch & chain your teeth were gold
you walked on a gold carpet America was gold to you
a gold boat drifted on a lake of gold
in the cabin gold men sat around a table
their smiles were gold & frozen like the gold fly
halfway between the ceiling & the floor
suspended in your dream of gold
becomes a gold pin for your tie the golden girl clips off
will let you stroke a gold tit in return
she smiles for the demonic newsmen
flashbulbs shatter the limits of your wakefulness
at midday   in forfeit of all love

ESTHER K. COMES TO AMERICA: 1931

The Wilderness: but otherwise
name of a cafeteria
where the two lovers drink tea
not speaking to each other
but sharing a world through separation:
1931: Esther K.
& Leo Levy
have met here at the end of a short life:
nothing begins as painfully
as the first step outside the glass door
the first sight of traffic
even the rumblings of the new subway under Houston Street:
all this happened in the course of ages
the priest tormented her & that was one
the governor broke into sighs & that was another
her mother became incontinent & that was the third
other events followed: fourth was the birth
of a child dead at childbirth
she massaged its hands but had to suck her own breasts:
stale odors: Leo Levy
going every morning to the chicken market
pursues his dream of power
Esther K. wonders: how was I ever trapped
inside this body?
in another life she would have been
a playgirl: not she
but someone else threw roses
in the Dnieper
danced on the drifting ice floe
to America
not someone else but she
opened the fly of the Shanghai dog-merchant
& greased his cock:
flesh erupting in the tropics
bewildering parrots

bathed in the mind of Esther K.
the traveler who crossed the Ganges
found Harlem
on the other side
the man with six fingers on one hand
had four on the other:
thus history repeated itself with marked rapidity
leading her to first meet
& then lose
Leo Levy: leading him
to polish his fingernails
with eggwhite
leading them both to read fortunes in earwax
to sell candy in turkish baths
& cotton in Canada
to remake "1931" as a talking movie:
what lovely dreams the world will have of Esther K.
said Leo Levy
I will make dreams for the world to have of Esther K.
& garments to wear in her image
I will comb her hair out until it reaches to Nicaragua
then will climb its length
& let it carry me to the top of a windy boat
sailing for Jerusalem: farewell!
the next price of almonds is a fair price
the poor under your window & the poor
around your table
will always be there: the bicyclists will too
but peddling backwards stumbling
against churches they will pretend
to drop behind: a crisis
the good life of the timid
beckons: it is a value
to be learned: a source of fortune
only too distant without refinement
both will grow sick & die
much later: separate beds
wait for them

chimeras dressed as chorus girls
to direct & love: his name
changed to Ben Messiah
hers to his: an aged couple
smelling of wet sheets
they will sometimes be holding hands
feeling how small the palms are: the Wilderness
has shrunk them: tomorrow
morning
was a lie:
a glass of tea:
maybe a bun with onions:
a suck:
two bitter almonds:
three half-chewed jelly slices:
a lemon
a lemon
a lemon
a lemon
a lemon
a lemon
etc

an inheritance   hardly dreamed of
they had carried it with them into the new city
during a time of ice Christmas mad December
pictures of their mothers covered the walls deep frames
held light in the corners under glass
he spoke with Gentiles more often these days working
the tops of shoes he dreamed of organizations
marched on Maydays from opposite ends of the town
the young men had come into another world
children with dogs & cats
sat on the high stoops some carved wood
others threw rocks at birds
waiting with mud between their toes they whistled
"the paradise of labor" was their song
a big round-bellied samovar hummed on the table
music was everywhere the walls were dancing
the cigarettes were English & smelled sweet to them
at night the young men slept together
not partners yet they were comrades
to each other   each left a sister
in their little town each shaved his head
& wore short jackets
dreamed past the Pripet Marshes to the Russian meadows
cities of pamphleteers
boulevards of orators
mechanics skilled in languages
& economics
naked proletarians in the woods of middle Europe
flowers with a single name
he brought back to his bed at night
walking from the shop the workers studyhouse
a comrade threw an arm around him
in the half light of blankets
he saw the ankle tighten something
like a web between the toes

his fingers pushed through his own hair
pulled back
he read his misfortune in the other's eyes
the evil urge their fathers
had called it   laughter in alleyways
battalions of pimps & thieves
invaded their classrooms stole all the girls
& shipped them to degradation
in Buenos Aires   only the young men
remained a hot breath
bothered his shoulder
the vision exploded into other rooms
comrades in a solitary dance
hasidic & lonely
circled the red-painted floor
the music slowed down freeing
the words to race ahead
the Great Name of God in his throat
choked him a stocking with hot salt
around his neck
his mother's lips touched his forehead again
carried in her apron kneaded
into her dough he sat
in the dust of an abandoned synagogue
a shoebox on his head
pendant of garlic cloves down to his waist
& a dead goose
he held a herring-head in one hand
an almsbox in the other
grandfathers walked over him & spat in his face
the international movement
trembled ranks broke
Lenin's beard floated on the Dnieper
torn from the dreamer his underwear
flew like a flag from the Tsar's palace
the young men were holding hands seated
on both sides of a long
table no a long bed

in uniforms with earlocks
still curled watching
the grandfather cut the bread of abundance
but hatless   telling them
"I am Karl Marx come to bring you to Paradise
"place the kiss on thy brother's lips in Paradise   red
"replica of the matriarchy's love for her children"
a veil
a kerchief over the head of their mother
(hairless)
the young men find no love in their bodies
but are always hopeful
tomorrow brings each one a small store
marriage the promise of revolution
the scientific study of history etcetera
into the snow of Poland he walks
as a straggler he comes down the center
of the road   on either side
rows of hooded men saintly processions
of workers to whom he speaks
in Yiddish
like an oriental Christ

THE MURDER INC. SUTRA

for Robert Kelly

Pincus Tavern
which Kelly passed
as schoolboy   den
of murderers or den of Jews
as murderers
no Benya Kriks he says
but bad guys simply
rotten
in the way of America
disposes   though I pretend
other Pincus Taverns meetingplaces of one-eyed
hand in caftan hardcocked
Jewish bandits
beautiful men of noses enlarged with purple veins
of still-curled earlocks from childhood
who dared to cross the border in three coats
watchbands laid out from wrist to shoulders
but beardless could whistle
lost messages in secret Jewish code
meaning
"the Tsar's asshole smells of vinegar" etcetera
& were obliged to wield knives   not only
to cut a notch off a salami
but slit a windpipe
spreading his blood across
the merchant's vest or seeing
pictures in it
of rabbis with hardons unheard of
in the secular world
real to their perceptions who were
brothel Jews & inn-
keepers
expert in management of taverns

where most would let the Polacks
drink but took a piece
themselves if pressed to it
even would suck each other off
in Polish prisons
from there to Brooklyn emanations
made the journey   sought
Golden Kingdoms
at the corner of Stone & Sutter
(Kelly thought) some lounged
in doorways   improbable murderous Litvaks
with names like Lepke   Gurrah   "Dutch Schultz"
        Rothstein   Lansky   Siegel
would drive wing'd cadillacs
with wraparound chrome exteriors of nineteen-thirty-one
to banquets on high holidays
eating turkey   chicken   goose with mushrooms
"a fish soup on which floated lakes of lemon juice"
drank velvety madeira booze from Canada cigars of J. P.
        Morgan sniffed cocaine sucked oranges
or dropped peels into their vodka
would wear a deluxe striped suit made of english navy
but with a head for business
Jews moved past el trains blasting tommy guns
other Jews made movies
ran after black girls   did a buck & wing
for Roman gangsters
toasted their mothers with hunky wines
that smelled of sun & bedbugs
of which the father of the dead man wrote in journal
"my child brings solace to a heavy heart
"his intense physicality
"not Jewish truly but tendering a dream of
"strength   resilience   broken promises
"a horsecock strapped between his legs
"in tribute   & my secret joy too
"seeing his dead frame surrounded
"by a thousand blossoms roses of old Poland

"a choir like the Warsaw Synagogue
"led by Sirota   bursts into songs of angels
"flashbulbs from fifty cameras pop
"blinding the humble button operators workers
"in black jackets & silk lapels some
"with yellow shoes   milk-stained wives   outclassed
"outdistanced by that stud in coffin
"whose hair pasted back still smells of
"whorehouse evenings along Atlantic Avenue
"not Moldavanka mad Odessa nights
"remembered the enforcers lift his coffin
"sweat stains the armpits of orange-colored suits
"strawberry vests   blue leather shoes
"& under the shirtcuff of the murdered son
"a diamond-studded bracelet"   thus
Babel or an uncle
might have written though the flesh
retreats from these as other
killers Jews who frightened the round-cheeked schoolboy
with gangster visions   of concrete
bodies into Catskill lakes
their fathers stood above & threw
lint from old pockets into
praying for joy   deliverance
from America the beautiful
oppressor riding in white convertible
up streets of Brownsville
the eagle of the golden States hooked on his arm
& hungry   diving
on faces that he hates
of Jew & Gentile
first searches their hearts for "freedom"
& the happy buck

PORTRAIT OF A JEW OLD COUNTRY STYLE

visitor to warsaw
           old man with open fly
      flesh girls could suck
                mothers would die to catch sight of
sometimes would pass your door
           his song was
      a generation is a day, time floweth
coldly he blew his nose
reached a hand around his high round waist
      money was pinned to caftan
        aches & pains
a jew's a jew he says
love brings him to the words he needs
           but sadly
    no
        I cannot stay
        for breakfast loving
        the taste of duck eggs loving
        little rolls & butter
        loving cereals in metal pans
he tells them
      all we touch is love
      & feeds us
this is a portrait of a jew old country style
the gentile will fail to understand
the jew come on better days will run from it
how real
the grandfathers become

      my grandfather the baker son of bakers
      YOSEL DOVID ben SHMIEL
      who was a hasid at the court in Rizhyn
      came to U. S. A. circa 1913
      but found the country godless
      tho he worked in leather

shoes were the craft all our friends
got into first
like his brother-in-law we called
THE UNCLE
I remember in a basement shop
somewhere "downtown"
bent over shoes he stitched
how many years would pass
till nineteen-fifty maybe
when I saw him last
his lungs gone in east bronx tenement
he slept behind a curtain
seeing me he thought
I was my brother   old & crazy
he was the oldest jew I knew
my grandfather had died
in nineteen-twenty
on the night my parents
ran to warsaw
to get married   my father
left for U.S.A. the next day
no one told him of his father's death
he would never be a talmudist
would go from shoes
to insurance
from insurance back to shoes
later an entrepreneur & bust
he was always clean
shaven   my grandmother
the religious one I mean
saw the first beard
I'd ever grown   got angry
"jews dont wear beards"
(she said) no
not in golden U.S.A.
the old man had fled from
to his Polish death

for which reason I deny autobiography
or that the life of a man
matters more or less
       "We are all one man"
       Cezanne said
I count the failures of these jews
as proof of their election
they are divine because they all die
                  screaming
          like the first
      universal jew
        the gentiles
           will tell you had some special deal

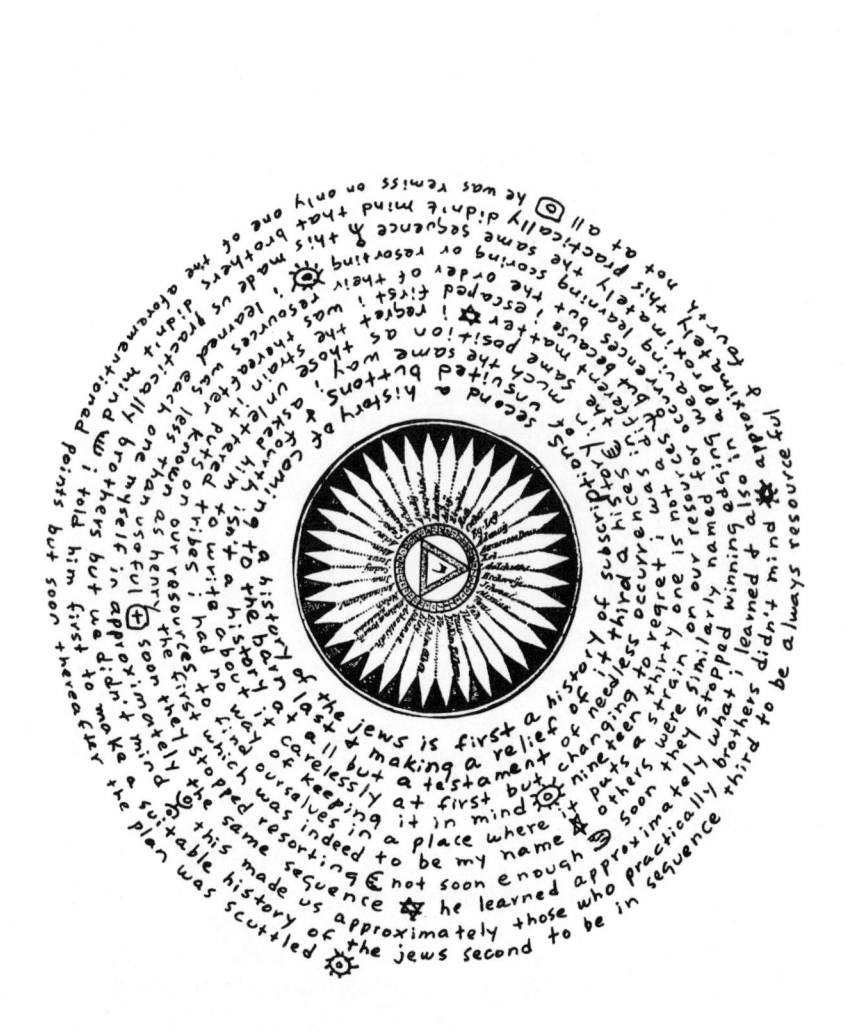

a history of the jews is first a relief or a history of subscription to it third a history of needless occurrences it was a strain on our resources at last & making a relief but a testament but at first changing to regret i was not a regret i was carelessly at first but nineteen thirty one others were similarly named soon they stopped winning adding and way of keeping it in mind puts a strain on our resources which was indeed to be my name not soon enough he learned approximately brothers didn't mind also i learned & also approt & this made us the same sequence the suitable history of approximately those who practically third to be in sequence plan was scuttled the jews second to be a always resourceful

A Book of Histories

HISTORY ONE

His childhood ambition had been to become a saint.

Hay covered the synagogue floor. It was an old synagogue, the ark carved by an Italian master. On one of the walls hung the matzo eaten at the end of the Passover seder. A metal vase filled with sand contained the prepuces of circumcised infants.

She told him she was Lilith & that if he let her go she would teach him all her names. The names she wrote down were

LILITH	ABITR	ABITO	AMORFO
KKODS	IKPODO	AYYLO	PTROTA
ABNUKTA	STRINA	KALI	PTUZA
	TLTOI-PRITSA.		

He told her he was Elijah.

. . . drinking beer & munching nuts

He had also warned me to be sure that the boiled milk had formed a skin.

long hose
½ shoes
sash about the loins
skullcap beneath a velvet hat
kerchief around neck
metal-rimmed spectacles

He loved to play chess & to make up riddles. "Three entered a cave & five came out"—the answer was Lot & his daughters. Or "what is that which is produced from the ground, yet man produces it, while its food is the fruit of the ground?" "A wick." Or "who was he that was born & died not?" Answer: Elijah & the Messiah.

someone had told me that if I were to light 40 candles & recite a secret incantation he would die

HISTORY TWO

The binding prevented the child from putting its toes into its mouth; also from touching its face with its fingers which may just before have touched its crotch or its toes

old fashioned gaberdine
a velvet hat with a high crown
½ boots, pantaloons & white socks

His ritual fringes reached below his knees.

The body was washed in warm water, scented with spices, & then a beaten egg was used as an additional cleansing agent.

Then one of the beadles would remove his boots & walk over the tablecloth in stocking feet, pouring wine for everyone.

Ordinarily she was a quiet girl, but suddenly she would begin to howl like a dog & to speak with a man's voice. Then she sang like a cantor, & her voice was as powerful as the roar of a lion.

"Arise, Rabbi Chisqiah, & stand in thy place & declare the worthiness of this part of the holy beard."

Rabbi Chisqiah arose, & began his speech & said, "I am my beloved's, & his desire is toward me."

. . . by their very exterior you could tell that these were no lovers of water & to your distress you often knew it with your eyes closed

how in Galicia, before a child was suckled, they placed part of a honeycomb in its cradle

The men of the congregation, having a quite different conception of the meaning of this anniversary, arrived with their pockets stuffed with thistles, which they proceeded to toss into each other's beards. When they ran out of thistles, they ripped the plaster from the walls & threw it

He had found an ancient commentary which declared that when Javan would be at war with Ishmael, the deliverance would come. And now he had heard, during a conversation in the ritual baths, that Russia & Turkey were on the point of war. Russia was of course Javan, & it had always been known that Turkey was descended from Ishmael, the son of Hagar, the handmaid of Sarah.

"It cannot be otherwise," the Rabbi muttered, & his excitement increased.

hernia
hemorrhoids

He took the torah scroll & hurled it to the ground, & then he had to fast for 40 days as a penance.

HISTORY THREE

They covered the mirrors with towels, drew the blinds, knocked over the chairs, broke the dishes, & stopped the clock. Then he put on a pair of felt slippers, to accompany the coffin.

"I eat only once a day, at four o'clock. For four years now."

. . . he burst into laughter finding that he had jewish hair, jewish eyes, a long jewish nose

an enema of lukewarm water & camomile, & sometimes added garlic

He drove off at top speed to New Court, where he arrived just before four o'clock in the afternoon. One of the porters immediately announced him to the head of the firm, whom he told that the Prime Minister wanted £4,000,000 the next day, & why. Baron Lionel picked up a muscatel grape, ate it, threw out the skin, & said, deliberately:

"What is your security?"

"The British Government," replied Corry.

Cutters
Jacket Pressers
Underpressers
Skirt Pressers
Skirt Basters
Skirt Finisher
Buttonhole Makers

While in one corner some stood at prayers, in other corners Jews ate & drank, drove bargains, argued & bought hot, peppered peas from an old woman who kept a supply under a mass of rags.

another tradition runneth thus: whiteness in whiteness & whiteness which includeth all other whiteness

There had been few Jews where he came from. In the course of the centuries their outward appearance had become Europeanized & had taken on a human look, so you might even have taken them for Germans. Then later, strolling through Vienna's inner city, he had suddenly encountered an apparition in a black caftan & black hairlocks. Was this a Jew? he thought. They hadn't looked that way in Linz. He observed the man furtively & cautiously, but the longer he stared, the more his first question assumed a new form: Was this a German?

. . . an awning of white silk or satin, supported on four poles & embroidered with the words, THE VOICE OF MIRTH & THE VOICE OF JOY, THE VOICE OF THE BRIDE-GROOM & THE VOICE OF THE BRIDE; also with flowers & green leaves . . .

Rabbi Shimeon began, & said: Woe unto him who extendeth his hand unto that most glorious supernal beard of the Holy Ancient One, the concealed of all.

This is the praise of that beard; the beard which is concealed & most precious in all its dispositions; the beard which neither the superiors have known; the beard which is the praise of all praise; the beard to which neither man, nor prophet, nor saint hath approached as to behold it.

The beard, whose long hairs hang down even unto the breast, white as snow; the adornment of adornments, the concealment of concealments, the truth of all truths.

. . . he was like a man who takes a ritual bath while holding an unclean reptile in his hand . . .

rice boiled in milk

HISTORY FOUR

There was the rabbi, for example, who said you mustn't
urinate in the snow on the Sabbath because it resembles
plowing . . .

Once, he told me, while studying the law in the Valley of
Genusan, he saw a man climbing a tree. The man found a
bird's nest in the tree, & taking the mother with the young
ones, he still departed in peace. He saw another man who
finding a bird's nest followed the Bible's command & took the
young only, allowing the mother to fly away—& yet a serpent
stung him as he descended & he died. "Now," he said, "where
is the Bible's truth & promises? Is it not written, 'And the
young thou mayest take to thyself, but the mother thou shalt
surely let go, that it may be well with thee & thou mayest live
many days.' Now, where is the long life to this man who
followed the precept, while the one who transgressed it is
unhurt?"

Their fur coats, old, & fur hats, older, made a pile on a chair.
Nails on the wall were the hangers, but chairs were better.
Around the talkers in the café were bits of lemon, crumbs of
cake, wetted lumps of sugar.

The doctor said: "I was told many times about women who
wake their husbands up in the middle of the night—& then all
she needs to come is for her husband to move near her."

two quadrangular diapers, one warm one of flannel, the other of linen, & a quadrangular piece of waterproof oilcloth. also a pillow stuffed with feathers

When her oldest son was 2½ years old, they went to the park for a walk. She led him, holding his hand. Whenever the child saw a small or large puddle he encircled it very carefully, in order not to soil his shoes. She always paid a lot of attention to the cleanliness of her boys.

In the women's rooms, where the bride was being prepared for the ceremony, it was cool & spacious. Girls danced together, lifting up the ends of their ballooning skirts; or else they stopped & talked affectedly with the musicians, trying to make their Yiddish sound like German.

awkward in her emotion she had slipped her face under the man's beard & left it buried there . . . her hands were clasped at the small of his back. As he dared a timid caress, barely sensual, on Judith's white neck, a question crossed his mind: Does God, blessed be his name, wish the death of infants?

With a sudden gesture, partly of shyness, partly the result of long training, he covered his eyes in order not to look at a woman, stepped aside, & murmured: "Good evening."

. . . the gutters, where dead horses lay for days or until a special truck came along to haul them off . . .

They conducted the queen to Solomon, who had gone to sit in a house of glass, to receive her. The queen was deceived by an illusion. She thought the king was sitting in water, & as she stepped across to him she raised her garment to keep it dry. On her bared feet the king noticed hair, & said to her: "Thy beauty is the beauty of a woman, but thy hair is masculine; hair is an ornament to a man, but it disfigures a woman."

And the sages said: "Make for me an opening as wide as the eye of a needle, & I shall make an opening for you as wide as the door of a chamber."

. . . later he was also nicknamed the Dancer of God

HISTORY FIVE

He wore a hat in the rabbinic style, but his alpaca jacket reached only to his knees, in the German fashion.

His trousers were striped, his boots glistened.

But he also had white earlocks.

Very frequently he would purify himself in the ritual bath: he would learn by heart & repeat the fantastic names of angels: & he would often deprive himself of meals.

When he was a child he had pictured God as living in the

moon. You know—he said—the face in the moon. There was a saying that God looks down from the moon, & he had pictured him that way.

The hut in which he lived was ice-cold. The windows were stopped up with cushions, & the smoke of the kitchen had blackened the walls. Wild mushrooms & toadstools sprouted on the dank, earthen floor. His second wife, a lean, haggard woman, sat on a low chair, pushing her hanging breast against a baby's mouth, & crying:
"Suck, draw, draw the life out of me!"

whenever he saw his own excreta he threw up

Moreover he spied a skull floating on the face of the water, he said to it: "For drowning others you were drowned; & in the end those who drowned you will be drowned."

The tsaddik shut himself up in his room, & it was said that the floor was covered with dust & never swept. Large mice used to run around, & old ugly grey frogs jumped in dark corners. The lonesome tsaddik treated them like well-groomed dogs. His disciples said that the frogs & mice were the souls of sinful, deceased hasidim.

Among them was one young beggar, supposedly released from an insane asylum, with a very beautiful & strong tenor voice. Whenever someone refused him charity he would intone the prayer for the dead at the top of his lungs. People stricken with awe gave him what he wanted & ran away.

"When I was born," he told George Cornwallis-West late in life, "I was so beautiful that my co-religionists took me for the Messiah. But they wouldn't think so now, would they?" he added ruefully.

Sleeping that night on the floor of a damp country synagogue, he had been awakened suddenly by a sound of distant singing. He followed it across the room to the great wooden ark of the covenant, whose doors swung open as he reached them. Inside he saw a blue light dancing before the scrolls of the law, & a woman's voice sang loudly: "I Am Afire with Love." It was the most beautiful thing he had ever seen.

not a mere fortuitous aggregation of individuals but a sacred society—a self-dedicated "kingdom of priests"

HISTORY SIX

She would drive off to the Odessa quarries, sit drinking tea with Jews at the Bear Café, buy smuggled goods on the waterfront. . . .

But the serious cafés were usually up one flight—on Division

Street, Allen Street, Orchard Street, Canal Street, or on Chatham Square.

he was wearing a brown jacket, cream-colored pants, & raspberry-red shoes

Machines, needles, thread, pressing cloth, oil, sponges . . . often the workers brought their own machines, as well as the needles & thread.

When they saw her in the distance, mothers would exclaim, "The demon!" & would pull their children into the house. Under their breath they muttered: "Salt in your eyes! Pepper in your nose!"

also cafés for domino players who drank nothing alcoholic & seldom talked

Two chinamen in bowler hats, holding loaves of bread under their arms, stood on the corner of Sadoraga Street. With their frosty nails, they marked off slivers of the loaf to lure the passing Jewish prostitutes. The women passed by them in a silent procession.

There was the Odessa Café on East Broadway. . . . Others were called Krakow, Moscow, Kiev, Lublin, & Warsaw. . . .

He brought two seamen along with him—an Englishman & a Malay—& the three of them dragged a case of contraband goods from Port Said into the yard. The case was heavy & they dropped it & out tumbled some cigars entangled in Japanese silk.

. . . the Rutgers Street Public Bath

He borrowed a comb & a necktie from an obliging detective, dusted off his shoes & faced the press, his usual, debonair self.

. . . bohemian cafés . . . noisy with dancers & accordionists

His ideals of life resolved themselves into money to spend, beautiful women to enjoy, silk underclothes, & places to go in style.

After dinner he settled in an armchair & opened a thin volume. His gangster friend had recommended *The Prince* as a way of gaining insight into the Italian mind.

"& Joseph will get a first class funeral—there'll be six horses like six lions, & two carriages for the wreaths, & the choir from the Brodsky synagogue, & Minkovsky in person will sing over your late son."

green horn
maki
griner
griner tukes

—How old were you when your mother stopped punishing
you?

—When I was old enough to defend myself—then she stopped.
I must have been about 16.

—Did she ever spank you?

—She *beat* me, & she threw things at me, & she hit me with
sticks, & she punched me, & she pulled my hair.

With an ancient Spanish dagger—none from Sicily was avail-
able—Trafficante cut his left wrist, allowed the blood to flow,
& wet his right hand in the crimson stream. Then he held up
the bloody hand.

"So long as the blood flows in my body," he intoned sol-
emnly, "do I, Santo Trafficante, swear allegiance to the will
of Meyer Lansky & the organization he represents. If I violate
this oath, may I burn in hell forever."

Tourine witnessed the signature with an X in ink. Sam
Tucker produced a band-aid, & the two Mafia leaders hurried
out.

. . . a play called *Demented America*—his final play

HISTORY SEVEN

" . . . During the second week the power became so strong in me that I couldn't manage to write down all the combinations of letters wch automatically spurted out of my pen. . . . When I came to the night in wch this power was conferred on me, & Midnight had passed, I set out to take up the Great Name of God, consisting of 72 Names, permuting & combining it. But when I had done this for a little while, the letters took on the shape of great mountains, strong trembling seized me & I could summon no strength, my hair stood on end, & it was as if I were not in this world. Then something resembling speech came to my lips & I forced them to move. I said: 'This is indeed the spirit of wisdom.'"

a head of a carp wrapped in cabbage leaves

Sometimes it happened that during the merchant's travels in the forests a young peasant woman would wait on him, the wife of some innkeeper: she would smile up at him as she drew the long boots off his feet before he went to bed: she would beg him to raise her husband's pay. Then he did not say no: nor did he refuse to let her kiss his hand out of gratitude when he had put out the light.

. . . picking cucumbers out of a barrel of brine

If any one came within ten feet of him during prayer or before it, the rabbi would shout words like "cattle" or "robbers"

& would sometimes slip off his belt & strike whoever was in his way.

. . . in the evening i brought her a white loaf as well as a dark one . . . also poppy seed rolls i baked myself . . . i thieved because of her & swiped everything i could lay my hands on . . . macaroons . . . raisins . . . almonds . . . cakes . . . i hope i may be forgiven for stealing from the saturday pots the women left to warm in the baker's oven . . . i would take out scraps of meat . . . a chunk of pudding . . . a chicken leg or head . . . a piece of tripe . . . whatever I could nip quickly . . . she ate & became fat & handsome . . .

Not only the gateway, the entire courtyard was filled with obstacles. Servant girls sang, & Reb Moishe stopped his ears, for the voice of woman leads to lewdness. The sound of gramophones came thru open windows, & sometimes a troop of magicians & acrobats gave a performance in the courtyard; a half-naked girl, wearing short breeches & a beaded jacket walked on her hands. Every step of the way was fraught with danger. Servants sat on the stairs, grating horse-radish & slicing onions. All the world's females seemed to be waylaying Reb Moishe, trying to deflect him from the narrow path of righteousness & lead him to Gehenna. But Reb Moishe carried his weapons—his walking stick. He closed his eyes & pounded the stone flags with his stick.

vodka & currant cake

Zanvl took hold of the bag; then with the swiftness of a young gypsy he lifted the door off the hinges. Warm steam beat into his face. He took out the whiskey, made the horses drunk, & put shoes on their feet. Then he led them softly out of the stable.

We used to make holes in the sand with the heels of our boots. All the holes had to be approximately the same size. Then we would all piss into these holes. The one who filled his hole first was the winner.

Every morning he went from door to door after he had pre-pared the synagogue. He tapped on the shutters with his wooden hammer & called out weakly: "Jews, rise! It is time to serve God."

a silken man

he had completely incarnated himself into a sacred lemon

Cokboy

COKBOY

saddlesore I came
a jew among
the indians
vot em I doink in dis strange place
mit deez pipple mit strange eyes
could be it's trouble
could be   could be
(he says) a shadow
ariseth from his buckwheat
has tomahawk in hand
shadow of an axe inside his right eye
of a fountain pen inside his left
vot em I doink here
how vass I lost tzu get here
am a hundred men
a hundred fifty different shadows
jews & gentiles
who bring the Law to Wilderness
(he says) this man
is me   my grandfather
& other men-of-letters
men with letters carrying the mail
lithuanian pony-express riders
the financially crazed Buffalo Bill
still riding in the lead
hours before avenging the death of Custer
making the first 3-D movie of those wars
or years before it
the numbers vanishing in kabbalistic time
that brings all men together
& the lonely rider
saddlesore
is me   my grandfather
& other men of letters
jews & gentiles entering

the domain of Indian
who bring the Law to Wilderness
in gold mines & shaky stores
the fur trade heavy agriculture
ballots bullets barbers
who threaten my beard your hair
but patronize me
& will make our kind the Senator from Arizona
the champion of their Law
who hates us both
but dresses as a jew one day an indian
the next a little christian shmuck
vot em I doink here
dis place is maybe crazy
has all the letters going backwards
(he says) so who can read the signboards
to the desert
who can shake his way out of the woods
ford streams the grandmothers
were living near
with snakes inside their cunts
teeth maybe
maybe chainsaws
when the Baal Shem visited America
he wore a shtreiml
the locals all thought he was a cowboy
maybe from Mexico
"a cokboy?"
no a cowboy
I will be more than a credit to my community
& race
but will search for my brother Esau among these redmen
their nocturnal fires I will share
piss strained from my holy cock
will bear seed of Adonoi
& feed them visions
I will fill full a clamshell
will pass it around from mouth to mouth

we will watch the moonrise
through each other's eyes
the distances vanishing in kabbalistic time
(he says) the old man watches
from the cliffs a city
overcome with light
the man & the city disappear
he looks & sees another city
this one is made of glass
inside the buildings stand
immobile statues
brown-skinned faces
catch the light
an elevator
moving up & down
in the vision of the Cuna *nele*
the vision of my grandfather
vision of the Baal Shem in America
the slaves in steerage
what have they seen in common
by what light their eyes
have opened into stars
I wouldn't know
what I was doing here
this place has all the letters going
backwards a reverse in time
towards wilderness
the old jew strains at his gaberdine
it parts for him
his spirit rushes up the mountainside
& meets an eagle
no an iggle
captains   commanders   dollinks   delicious madmen
murderers opening the continent up to exploitation
cease & desist (he says)
let's speak (he says)
feels like a little gas down here (he says)
(can't face the mirror without crying)

& the iggle lifts him
like an elevator
to a safe place above the sunrise
there gives a song to him
the Baal Shem's song
repeated without words for centuries
"hey heya heya" but translates it
as "yuh-buh-buh-buh-buh-buh-bum"
when the Baal Shem (yuh-buh) learns to do a bundle
what does the Baal Shem (buh-buh) put into the bundle?
silk of his prayershawl-bag beneath
cover of beaverskin above
savor of esrog fruit within
horn of a mountaingoat between
feather of dove around the sides
clove of a Polish garlic at its heart
he wears when traveling
in journeys through kabbalistic forests
cavalry of the Tsars on every side
men with fat moustaches yellow eyes & sabers
who stalk the gentle soul
at night through the Wyoming steppes
(he says) vot em I doink here
I could not find mine het
would search the countryside on hands & knees
until   behind a rock in Cody
old indian steps forth
the prophecies of both join at this point
like smoke a pipe is held
between them dribbles through their lips
the keen tobacco
"cowboy?"
cokboy (says the Baal Shem)
places a walnut in his handkerchief & cracks it
on a boulder each one eats
the indian draws forth a deck of cards
& shuffles
"game?"

they play at wolves & lambs
the fire crackles in the pripitchok
in a large tent somewhere in America
the story of the coming-forth begins

COKBOY Part Two

comes a brown
wind curling from
tense tissues sphincter
opened over the whole continental
divide & shot the people up
plop plop a little girl emergeth
she with the beaver tits nose furry
eyes of the Redman's
Sabbath
gropes down the corridor
(sez) hallo doctor
got a hand to spare?
doctor sez hokay
—yas doctor
hand up her bush
he pulls
a baby   howling
in lamplight a little Moses
now the Cacique's daughter laugheth
—oh doctor not so-o hard
so hard America is born
so hard the Baal Shem dreams about it
200 years later
in Vitebsk
(he was in correspondence with Wm Blake
appeared on Peckham Rye
—yes fully clothed!—

& was his angel)
angel says his mother
smiling proud
she sees his little foot
break through
her crotch an itching
races up her ribs
America is born
the Baal Shem is a beaver
(happened while the Indian talked
chanted behind Cody
the mad jew slid to life
past pink styrofoam snow of her body's
channels
the freaky passageways
unlit unloved
like gums of an old woman
teeth were ripped from
ages gone) into
another kind of world
he hurtles
does reawaken in the female swamp
a beaver amongst the rushes
—momma!—calls the Baal Shem
—mommeleh!
vot em I doink here
I hev become mine beard
(he says) the blind world shines on him
water runs through his mouth
down belly it is dark
a darkness (fur is dark
& hides the skin & blood
a universal fur
but leaves one hole
to open from the body's
darkness pushing
into light)
erupts

like great cock of the primal beings
red & smooth like copper
of the sun's red eye at night
old Beaver lugs it in his hand
I am myself   my grandfather
(he sings) my name is Cokboy
—COKBOY, understand?
I leave my grandmother in the female swamp
will be the Great Deliverer someday yuh-buh-bum
even might find a jar of honey might stick my prick in my
    prick might tingle might it not tickle me the bees find out
    about it & sting the knob it grows a second a dozen or so
    knobs along its length are maybe 30 knobs
so what's the use I ask maybe will try again I drag it red &
    sore behind me so vulnerable I have become in this hot
    climate shitting & farting shooting marbles was opening
    my mouth & coming in it
the blackbird shits o not so fast love into my hat my eyes turn
    white wood-lilies are growing from them a slavic birth I
    can't deny so tender in my eyes tender the native turds
    come floating
& across America in an outrage uselessly I shout against the
    Sun you are no longer my father Moon you are no longer
    my mother I have left you have gone out jaunty with cock
    slung over shoulder this is the journey your young men
    will take
(says Beaver) makes it to the hut where that old woman lives
    apron over her belly carp in oven maybe fried bread fat
    fat little mother don't mind if I drop a stone onto your
    brains your daughters be back later little hot girls I ride
    on pretending I was you I suck their ears & scream o put
    me lower down love o my cock inside
& have to cool it
I cool it
in waters where a princess
daughter of a chief
went bathing
lethal & innocent the cock

has found its mark
(his train has reached Topeka
Custer is dead)
& enters the bridegroom's quarters
darkness her flesh prepared for it
by new moon
in her abdomen a sliver
grows
a silver dollar over Barstow
lighting the Marriage of America
in kabbalistic time
(says Cokboy) you are the daughter of
the mountain
now will I take thee to my father's tribe
to do the snake dance
o jewish feet of El go crazy
in his mind
o
El
o
Him
I carry in my knapsack
dirty pictures land grants
(but further back her people
gun for him
how should they feel
seeing their daughter in arms of
Cokboy
—C-O-C-K, understand?—)
thou art become my Father's bride
are wedded to (ugh) Christian god
forever
bye bye I got to run now
engagements await us in Salt Lake City
industry riseth everywhere
arrows strike concrete
never shall bruise my sweetie's flesh
(says Cokboy) on horse

up river he makes his way
past mining camps Polacks were panning gold in
& other pure products of America
o prospectors o Anglo Saxons
baby-faced dumplings who pacified the west
with gattling guns with bounties for hides of babes
mothers' vulvas made baseballs to their lust
o bringers of civilization heros heros
I will fight my way past you who guard the sacred border
last frontier village of my dreams
with shootouts tyrannies
(he cries) who had escaped the law
or brought it with him
how vass I lost tzu get here
was luckless
on a mountain & kept from
true entry to the west true paradise
like Moses in the Rockies who stares at California spooky in
     the jewish light
of horns atop my head great orange freeways of the mind
America disaster
America disaster
America disaster
America disaster
where he can watch the sun go down
in desert
Cokboy asleep (they ask)
awake (cries Cokboy)
only his beard has left him
like his own   his grandfather's
ghost of Ishi was waiting on the crest
looked like a Jew
but silent
was silent in America
guess I got nothing left to say

INDEX OF TITLES